California Gothic

California Gothic

The Dark Side of the Dream

Charles L. Crow

ANTHEM PRESS

Anthem Press
An imprint of Wimbledon Publishing Company
www.anthempress.com

This edition first published in UK and USA 2024
by ANTHEM PRESS
75–76 Blackfriars Road, London SE1 8HA, UK
or PO Box 9779, London SW19 7ZG, UK
and
244 Madison Ave #116, New York, NY 10016, USA

British Library Cataloguing-in-Publication Data
A catalogue record for this book is available from the British Library.

Library of Congress Cataloging-in-Publication Data
A catalog record for this book has been requested.
2023945339

ISBN-13: 978-1-83998-379-5 (Pbk)
ISBN-10: 1-83998-379-5 (Pbk)

Cover Credit: *Unidentified Woman*, by Jonathan Crow

This title is also available as an e-book.

For Cynthia, My California Girl.

CONTENTS

LIST OF FIGURES

PREFACE

California, the land of perpetual sunshine, might seem the least Gothic of American regions. Where are the "deep and gloomy wrongs" (in Hawthorne's phrase) that are obviously part of New England's heritage or that of the South? New England's witchcraft trials, its isolated villages, and its brutal winters are obviously the stuff of the Gothic. The South has the legacy of slavery and its aftermath, its tangled racial bloodlines, swamps, crumbling mansions, and the legend of the Lost Cause, all of which have nourished some of the most profound and disturbing American literature, much of it Gothic.

Instead, the Golden State has the California Dream. This complex of ideas and aspirations needs to be unpacked and has historical roots that anticipate the European discovery of North America. For Americans from the nineteenth century to the present, the dream has evolved continuously, as documented by Kevin Starr's magisterial eight-volume history. The California Dream has meant a variation on the American Dream, restated with urgency, since, as Joan Didion observed, "things had better work here, because here ... is where we run out of continent" (p. 172). At a minimum, it evokes an aspiration to begin again and live a fulfilling life in a welcoming climate and landscape. Obviously, the California Dream is now threatened by ecological disaster and global pandemics, both of which were long anticipated by California authors, as well as the failure of its inhabitants to become worthy of its landscape.

The contention of this book is that the California Dream is also a source of the Gothic, like the myth of the Old South, and that the California Gothic has much to say about the situation of America and the world. We need to explore this complex idea and see what was left out as it was constructed. The California dream has required the suppression of other narratives, and these alternate realities and lost stories, in the nature of the suppressed, return as the uncanny nightmares of the California Gothic.

Californians built their civilization in the space of a few decades in places where "they shouldn't have" (p. 3), as Marc Reisner reminds us: in earthquake zones, on the interface with wild lands subject to fire, and far from fresh water.

The landscape has been both inspiring and threatening. One paradox of California's civilization is that it is inherently fragile and that it was built by pushing aside the oldest peoples in the Americas, who had lived in a stable relationship with the land for over ten thousand years.

Because of California's fragility, there has always been a fear of its collapse. One touchstone of this study is the series of paintings by Thomas Cole, "The Course of Empire," which illustrates, in five panels, the development, triumph, and destruction of a civilization. This fear of downfall is shown as early as Ambrose Bierce's story "An Inhabitant of Carcosa" and is central to the later chapters on Disease Gothic and Ecogothic.

Among the recurring patterns and throughlines of this study, readers will note two historical figures. John Muir, more than anyone else, celebrated the California landscape as a place of beauty, renewal, and refuge. In works by later authors, he is evoked as a symbol of what has been lost. The second figure, a contemporary of Muir and such writers as Jack London, is Ishi, the last survivor of his tribe and the last Indigenous Californian to fall under the control of white authority. Ishi is a complex figure in the California imaginary, focusing both guilt and longing. The destruction of California's tribes and the suppression of their stories are the beginning of California Gothic. The desire to achieve, or recover, a lost Indigenous kinship with the land and to find a true home here is a great theme of California literature.

We begin, then, with the land and the tales explorers and settlers have spun about it. Chapter 1 recalls the Spanish novel that gave California its name and looks in detail at the tragedy of the Donner-Reed Party (1867–68) and the burning of the town of Paradise in 2018. These events qualify the romantic view of the California landscape celebrated by John Muir and foreshadow the Gothic tales of disaster seen in later chapters.

Chapter 2 shows that the Gothic has been present from the beginning of California fiction. Ambrose Bierce's first published short story, "The Haunted Valley," is a California Gothic, and he would recur to California settings throughout his career, down to one of his last major short stories, "The Death of Halpin Frayser." His younger friend Emma Francis Dawson, an unfairly neglected writer of real talent, helped to establish the new city of San Francisco as a site of urban Gothic fiction.

Chapter 3 turns from urban to coastal Gothic. We trace a bohemian tradition that was begun by a group centering on George Sterling at Carmel, which celebrated a simple life of artistic creation on the beach and wooded headlands. We recognize in the Carmel Bohemians the origin of a style that would resurface in the Beats and in the creative flash of the 1960s. The "Matter of the Sixties," indeed, forms an important focus of this study. On our way from turn-of-the-century Carmel to the remote "Lost Coast" in the north, we encounter writers, celebrated and neglected, from Jack London, Mary Austin, and Nora May French to John Steinbeck, Thomas Pynchon, Denis Johnson, and Kem Nunn.

California's climates, dry desert interiors and mild coastal Mediterranean, have promised health to refugees from Eastern cities and the tropical, fever-ridden South. Chapter 4 explores the failure of that hope. After all, many immigrants ultimately found early death, not health, in the Golden State. California writers present victims of loathsome diseases, from syphilis (the nineteenth century offered no cure) and AIDs to imagined global pandemics that might sweep away most of humanity. Plague, like war, is one of the great forces that can end civilization and bring desolation, the final stage of Cole's Course of Empire. Frank Norris wrote the first syphilis Gothic (*Vandover and the Brute*), and Jack London wrote the first California novel of plague apocalypse (*The Scarlet Plague*), which George Stewart revisited in *Earth Abides*. In *I Am Legend*, Richard Matheson destroys humanity through a vampire plague, while the vampire-as-disease trope is given another twist in the movie *Blade*. As in American literature from the beginning (see C. B. Brown's *Arthur Mervyn*) to the present, physical disease is often linked to political and social corruption. If, as Susan Sontag said, disease is a metaphor, the several diseases, real and imaginary, in these works offer insights into the social anxieties and disfunctions of their times.

From disease, Chapter 5 turns to crime: the noir tradition in cinema and the California hard-boiled crime novel, which often provided the movies' stories. Our approach is through the femme fatales, who, I argue, can be seen as imbodying Poe's "Imp of the Perverse." Her presence makes each of the narratives Gothic, as in Raymond Chandler's *The Lady in the Lake*, Alfred Hitchcock's *Vertigo*, David Lynch's *Mulholland Drive* (2001), Walter Moseley's *The Devil in a Blue Dress* (1990), James Elroy's *The Black Dahlia* (1987), and Thomas Pynchon's *Inherent Vice* (2009). The true crime stories of Los Angeles provide essential background for several works: the murder of Elizabeth Short (the "Black Dahlia"), and the Manson Family murders of Sharon Tate, and four others. With Pynchon's novel, we encounter again the "Matter of the Sixties," a recurring theme.

In the Chapter 6, we return to the apocalypse, the end of all—pictured or anticipated—through human destruction of the natural environment. This would mean the ironic end of the California Dream, which always promised a healthy interaction with the natural world.

Octavia Butler's *Parable of the Sower* (1993) shows the burning of Los Angeles and a desperate flight to escape it, while Claire Vaye Watkins' *Gold Fame Citrus* (2015) shows California destroyed by a drought, which sends refugees east in an ironic inversion of the 1930s dust bowl. In contrast to these novels of the near future, Lydia Millet's Ecogothic trilogy, *How the Dead Dream* (2008), *Ghost Lights* (2011), and *Magnificence* (2012), is set in the present and is a mediation on the failed relationship of humans with the animal world. The final novel of the sequence is a haunted house novel, which contains, in true uncanny fashion, a secret in its basement.

Readers of this study may be aware of Bernice M. Murphy's recently published book, *The California Gothic in Fiction and Film* (2022). The gestation of our studies overlapped considerably, and Professor Murphy and I, both members of the International Gothic Association, were aware of each other's work in progress. We briefly exchanged ideas and once spent a pleasant hour conversing over coffee in Berkeley. Professor Murphy and I share an approach and many attitudes about California; she offers a European perspective, and I that of one native to the state. However, there is very little overlap between the works discussed. That this is so testifies to the richness of the field. Readers of both books will discover other authors, texts, films, and indeed, whole areas of California experience still to be studied. The gates of California Gothic studies now stand ajar, inviting further exploration.

ACKNOWLEDGEMENTS

The five paintings in *The Course of Empire* series by Thomas Cole are reproduced by permission of the New York Historical Society.

Figure 0.1 Thomas Cole, The Savage State.

Figure 0.2 Thomas Cole, The Arcadian or Pastoral State.

Figure 0.3 Thomas Cole, Consummation of Empire.

Figure 0.4 Thomas Cole, Destruction.

Figure 0.5 Thomas Cole, Desolation.

Chapter 1

THE MAGIC ISLAND

Never take no cut-offs, and hurry along as fast as you can.
—Virginia Reed, survivor of the Donner Tragedy

California existed in the minds of Europeans as a literary construct before the idea was attached to a physical space.

The New World of the Americas was, at first, for Europeans, a constellation of islands. The islands putatively "discovered" by Columbus were seen through the lens of European tales and theories, both ancient and modern: the Terrestrial Paradise, Atlantis, Utopia, and fantasies about Amazon warriors. As stories came back to Europe of new lands in the Atlantic and Caribbean, they evoked yet more island fantasies. Shakespeare's *The Tempest* (ca. 1610) was inspired in part by reports of Bermuda. Island by island, Spanish and Portuguese explorers were hoping they had reached the fabled Spice Islands of Asia. When it was clear that South America was a continent, not an island, they rounded its southern tip and sailed on, still hoping for island riches.

When Hernán Cortéz reached the tip of Baja California in 1536, he thought he had discovered another island. Cortéz named this island *California* after a recent romance novel that was the latest version of European island fantasies. *Las Sergas de Esplandían* (1510), by Garci Ordóñez de Montalvo, imagined an island ruled by the Amazon queen Califia, and peopled by deeply tanned athletic women clad mainly in gold jewelry. Thus was this existing literary idea of California (and the California Girl) was grafted onto the physical space.

The long dispute over whether California was an island or not, as Dora Beale Polk documents, began immediately and lasted—strangely—for about 200 years. Even though explorers in the 1500s had reached the mouth of the Colorado River at the top of the Sea of Cortez (the Gulf of California), Spaniards reluctantly gave up the belief in Island California, and kept producing maps that showed a link from the northern gulf, or the Colorado River, to the Pacific (Fig. 1.1). Finally, in 1747, Spanish king Ferdinand VI ended the dispute by proclaiming that "California is not an island" (p. 326).

Figure 1.1 Map of California as an Island.

This was long after Spaniards had reached the real spice islands of Asia and had established the first truly global trade networks, linking China through the Philippines to Mexico and Spain. California, finally understood as attached to North America, remained a backwater, and was the most remote and tenuous part of the Spanish empire. But as Polk notes, California in a sense remained an island still, geologically (because of plate tectonics), as well as ecologically and culturally (Polk 1991, 229–30).[1]

The California Frontier

California can be understood as a frontier in two senses: as the end point of western migration and as a contact zone of cultures and languages.

The word *frontier* is deeply embedded in American culture and is linked to other key American concepts, including *wilderness*, *progress*, and *pioneer*. The notion of the frontier as a westward-moving line crossing the continent was anticipated by Crèvecoeur in his *Letters from an American Farmer* (1782) and given its fullest expression by Frederick Jackson Turner in his lecture at the American Historical Association in Chicago in 1893, "The Significance of the Frontier in American History." According to the Turnerian frontier thesis, the distinctive fact about American culture is that every part of the continental United States has been crossed by the frontier, defined as the farthest advance of European civilization. Every point was once a wilderness, then was penetrated by hunters and trappers, then pioneers who settled and brought the wild land under cultivation, producing a rough democratic culture, and, finally, urban civilization.

Walt Whitman's poem "Facing West from California's Shores" (266–67) illustrates an elaboration of the Turnerian frontier thesis and links the movement of settlers across North America to the earlier *Völkerwanderung* of Slavic and Germanic tribes out of Asia and across Europe. Thus Whitman's speaker, "Facing West from California's shores" and looking toward Asia, completes a millennium-long odyssey. This belief, widely held among Americans, makes of western migration an inevitable historical force. Like the belief in progress, which was an American secular faith, the movement west was linked to democratic values, America's manifest destiny.

From the beginning, the American frontier has had a Gothic dimension. Facing west from the deck of the Mayflower (when the frontier was the beach), William Bradford saw a "desolate wilderness" that was the kingdom of Satan, filled with "wild beasts and wild men" (p. 75). The view of English settlers, especially the Puritans, was essentially Manichean, with opposed forces of light and darkness on either side of the frontier. The fine collection *Frontier Gothic*, edited by David Mogan et al., explores ways that the liminal zone of the frontier could also stand for other borderlands, such as that between conscious and unconscious, or reason and madness.

As a realm of the unknown, the wilderness had terrors that could threaten the body—the wild beasts and wild men, as well as starvation—but it presented an even greater threat. In crossing the line, the explorer risked becoming the dreaded other, becoming, in some sense, wild or savage, or a child of Satan. This fear underlies the Salem witchcraft trials and is the basis for early American Gothic novels, such as Charles Brockden Brown's *Edgar Huntly* (1799), in which the protagonist emerges from a cavern in which he has killed a wildcat and eaten it raw to engage in a series of battles with Indian warriors in which he becomes more savage and brutal than his antagonists. This fear of becoming savage, of not progressing but of sliding down the evolutionary scale, was always present in early California. In the 1850s, especially, when, as the title of J. S. Holliday's book aptly described, *The World Rushed In* (1981) and young men from around the world frantically scrambled for gold, civilization seemed for a time to have collapsed.

California complicated, and in some ways refuted, the Turner thesis of the frontier as a line of progress moving westward across the landscape. In California, settlement had leapfrogged across the Great Plains, the Rocky Mountains, the Great Basin, and the Sierra. In fact, settlers had come from all directions, arriving often by sea and including people—mostly men—of all races. The frontier had not always brought the benefits of European civilization imagined by Turner.

In Maxine Hong Kingston's *Tripmaster Monkey*, the protagonist Wittman Ah-Sing (a name to savor) stands at Coit Tower in San Francisco and recites Walt Whitman's "Facing West from California's Shores":

Facing West from California's shores,
Inquiring tireless, seeking what is yet unfound,
    I, a child, very old, over waves, toward the house
Of maternity, the land of migrations, look afar .... (p. 162)

Clearly, Wittman Ah-Sing, the child of migrants from Canton (like Kingston), sees Asia quite differently from Walt Whitman's imagined pioneer. For immigrants from China, California was not the magic island imagined by Europeans, nor was it the end of westering; it was the Gold Mountain, a land of opportunity in the East.

Contemporary scholars such as Annette Kolodny have replaced Turner's moving line with a new definition of a frontier as a contact zone where cultures and languages interact. Such a definition pushes California's frontier backward in time to the earliest contact between native peoples and Europeans. One of Cortez's lieutenants reached Baja California in 1534, and Francis Drake landed, presumably at the bay that now bears his name, in 1579, and, claiming the land for Queen Elizabeth, named it Nova Albion—New England. Throughout the next 200 years, Northern California was sometimes visited by Spanish ships riding the trade winds back from the Philippines, and artifacts from occasional wrecked ships, including Chinese goods, found their way into indigenous villages. In the south, trade routes with the Southwest and Mexico brought iron tools, horses, and—inevitably—diseases. In this sense, California was one of the oldest American frontiers and, with its great racial, ethnic, and linguistic diversity, is still a frontier.

California Uncanny

The Present Absence

According to recent anthropology work summarized by Ross Anderson, the indigenous peoples of California may be the first and oldest human settlers in the Americas. Arriving perhaps 13,500 years ago, they first made a home on the Channel Islands off present-day Santa Barbara. For native peoples, California also began as an island. They spread inland into a rich landscape replete with food resources. At the time of the European invasion of the "New World," California was the most populous region of what is now the United States (as it is again now). Yet California Indians are nearly invisible in the American imagination. Scholar Renée Bergland writes of the repression of the memory of native Americans and their uncanny reappearance, often in Gothic literature and film. Nowhere was the memory of native Americans more suppressed and deliberately erased than in California. Generations of California schoolchildren have learned about the California Missions, the system founded by Junipero Serra, without learning what happened to the Indians for whose benefit the missions were supposedly built. While most Americans know something about Sitting Bull and Crazy Horse, heroic figures of plains Indian resistance, few remember Captain Jack, the Modoc leader who held off an American Army for four months in 1873 in the lava beds north of Mount Lassen. Some may know Helen Hunt Jackson's sentimental romance *Ramona* (1884). Others may have read of the real Yahi, Ishi, the last of his tribe, who descended into Oroville in 1911 and was treated as a living museum piece by Berkeley anthropologists Alfred Kroeber and Thomas Talbot Waterman. All these examples amount to little in comparison to the Sioux and Cheyenne, to Crazy Horse and Sitting Bull and Chief Seattle, in the American imagination.

The erasure of California's abundant indigenous population through disease, displacement, and "Indian wars," a euphemism for explicit genocide, is among the gloomiest episodes of American history. It is not surprising that this history is seldom taught to fourth graders.

California Indians, I argue, are a *present absence* in the state, everywhere sensed if seldom seen. The subdivision built on an Indian burial ground is an obvious Gothic trope. More subtly, in literature and life, Californians, seeking a better relationship to their landscape, gropingly reproduce Native California. Recently, California Indian characters reappear in California literature, and often, as we will see, in Gothic tales, even as actual surviving tribe members, who have never entirely gone away, are acting to reclaim tribal lands.

Here is another version of the California Dream. In 1869, a prophet named Wodziwob appeared in the Great Basin among the Northern Paiutes. The prophet spread a religion that taught a return to the old ways and a ritual dance that would provide visions. If practiced correctly, the religion promised that an era of peace would descend. In some versions of the cult, the white invaders and their alien plants and stinking animals would roll up and disappear, leaving the purified land to its original inhabitants. The new religion quickly spread to and throughout California, where it still may influence some tribal communities. Whites called those who practiced the new cult "Ghost Dancers." They called themselves Dreamers (Akins and Bauer 2021, p. 154).

From Donner Lake to Paradise

As the nineteenth century ended, Californians found new ways to view and think about the state's abundant wilderness areas. In fact, the meaning of "wilderness," that key American concept, had radically changed from signifying the realm of Satan as defined by William Bradford and his Puritan successors. From its Manichean conception, which fit so well with the dark Romanticism of Brown, Hawthorne, Melville, and Poe, wilderness became, instead, a place of refuge and renewal. The chief theoretician of this change was Ralph Waldo Emerson, and his book *Nature* (1836) was its manifesto. Emerson's Transcendental view of nature was given a California application by the state's secular saint, John Muir, in such books as *The Mountains of California* (1894) and *The Yosemite* (1912). John Muir is, in my reading, the last great American romantic writer.

Muir's vision has been a force for good in preserving land from development, in the creation of Yosemite National Park, and, through his influence on Theodore Roosevelt, in shaping the National Park system. Muir's legacy today is carried on by his Sierra Club and the Wilderness Society, among other conservation groups.

Without disparaging these efforts, or their leadership in environmental issues, there always has been something wrong with the romantic vision of wilderness promoted by Muir. Wilderness, in this view, is empty. It is land from which the original "wild men" seen by Bradford have been erased. Yet the land, for native peoples, was never empty; in fact, it was never wilderness. According to Luther Standing Bear, "Only to the White man was nature a 'wilderness' and only to him was the land infested by 'wild' animals and 'savage' people" (Forbes 2003, p. 23). Consider the ironies in the name of a tract of forest south of Mt. Lassen now called the "Ishi Wilderness." Named to honor Ishi, it is the Ishi Wilderness because *Ishi is not there*, nor is his tribe, which was exterminated by white invaders. Ishi is an example of the indigenous Californian as a "present absence," everywhere felt but nowhere to be found.

Muir's vision was of a landscape that is essentially benign, which restores the soul of the city dweller. But California's natural world can be harsh and unforgiving, despite its beauty. The fabled four seasons of California—fire, flood, earthquake, and drought—always threaten to sweep away a fragile recent civilization. To these could be added epidemic disease, as a fifth threat. All have been made more dangerous by global human activity that extends beyond California.

Two tragedies bookend Californians' fraught relationship with their landscape: the ordeal of the Donner-Reed Party in 1846–47, and the burning of the town of Paradise in 2018.

Every Californian knows the story of the Donner-Reed Party, which was, as Kevin Starr puts it, "a phantasmagoria of horrors, including murder and cannibalism, that remains to this day a fixed and recurring statement of California as betrayed hope and dystopian tragedy (*California* 63)." Its significance as a foundational event in California history is heightened by the fact that it occurred simultaneously with the separation of California from Mexico. The Bear Flag Rebellion of May, 1846 and the raising of the American flag by U.S. sailors and Marines at Monterey (July 7) occurred while the Donner-Reed Party was making its way across the plains. When Californios under Andrés Pico defeated American forces at the Battle of San Pasqual on December 6, 1846, the Donner-Reed Party had been trapped in the snow for over a month.

Remarkably, the figure of James Reed unites both the creation of California as a state and the Donner tragedy, and thus, in a sense, both the hopeful and the Gothic visions of California's future. Reed had killed a fellow immigrant in a fight before the wagon train was trapped by snow and, rather than being hanged, as many urged, was forced to travel alone as an exile from the group. Crossing the Sierra just before winter's trap was sprung in early November, he frantically scoured central California for men and resources to rescue the immigrants, which included his wife and children. On January 2, 1847, Reed (who had military experience from the Black Hawk War in Illinois) participated in the Battle of Santa Clara. It was a minor skirmish, but it signaled the end of California's resistance to the American takeover.

Meanwhile, in the Sierra, the first acts of cannibalism were about to occur. A group of twelve men and five women, comprising most of the strongest immigrants, left Truckee Lake (now Donner Lake) in mid-December 1846. The group would be known as the "snowshoe party." Thirty-three days later, two men and all five women stumbled into the safety of Johnson's Ranch on the west side of the mountain. All had survived on human flesh. The women had eaten almost all the men.

Back in the squalid shelters in the snow the cattle were eaten, then hides and boots, and, at last, inevitably, the bodies of the dead. Teams of rescuers (one led by Reed) came in the spring, battling late snowstorms. When the second rescue party arrived in March 1847, they found scenes of horror, with "bits of human hair, many bones, and half-consumed fragment of limbs" scattered about. Perhaps the most nightmarish sight was that of children sitting upon a log, "their chins and breasts smeared bloodily as they innocently tore into the half-roasted heart and liver" (Stewart 1936, *Ordeal*, pp. 215–16).

When the last recovery team arrived later in March, they found only one survivor, Lewis Keseberg. The suspicion remains to this day that Keseberg murdered Tamsen Donner, the widow of George Donner (whom he also ate) to add to his larder. He continued to feast on Tamsen's remains even after supplies arrived, until he was prevented by his disgusted rescuers.

The Donner tragedy answers every definition of Gothic. Any reader of, for instance, George Stewart's fine history, *Ordeal by Hunger* (1936), will experience the horror of such scenes as that quoted above as something like the *uncanny* as defined by Sigmund Freud. The violation of taboos, the revelation of terrible deeds that should be kept hidden, the breaking of family bonds—it is all there.

So it was audacious for Alma Katsu to write a Gothic novel about the already Gothic Donner tragedy, to which she adds a supernatural element. In Katsu's retelling in *The Hunger* (2018), the Donner party's misfortunes, which began during its crossing of the Great Plains, were shaped by an evil spirit lodged in Lewis Keseberg. Though this evil is never named by Katsu, Keseberg is not a werewolf, but a *wendigo*—a monstrous being that has become increasingly important in both indigenous thought and in North American Gothic literature.[2]

The wendigo (the name has variants, including wétiko) was originally, according to eastern tribes, a cannibalistic monster that grows as it devours, never satisfying its appetite. In this tradition, a human who succumbs to greed and antisocial behavior could become a wendigo. This belief has been given a twist by contemporary indigenous authors like Jack D. Forbes, who argues that *"Columbus was a* wétiko, *that he was mentally ill or insane, the carrier of a terribly contagious psychological disease, the* wétiko *psychosis"* (Forbes 2003, p. 22, italics in the original). The wétiko or wendigo disease was spread across the continent, and "In California … the two greatest heroes of the establishment are John Sutter and Junipero Serra, both *wétikos*" (Forbes 2008, p. 23). In Alma Katsu's retelling of the Donner tragedy, then, the settlers crossing the Sierra were another vector of the wendigo disease. The insatiable greed of the Gold Rush, beginning almost immediately after Keseberg's arrival, confirms this diagnosis.[3]

If the Donner Party, wendigos or not, illustrates a Dark Romantic (i.e., Gothic) view of nature, and of human nature, the recent burnings of Paradise and other California communities bring us into the apocalyptic present, challenging comfortable beliefs that most Californians, until recently, held.

Some of the most desirable real estate in California has been at the wildland-urban interface, often in the foothills or mountains. This always has been fire-prone land, and major fires have been a feature of this landscape since the early twentieth century. In Southern California, Malibu and Santa Barbara, both areas with expensive estates, have burned repeatedly, so that Mike Davis has made "The Case for Letting Malibu Burn" (95–147). In Northern California, the 1991 Tunnel Fire destroyed some 3,500 homes in the scenic hillsides above Berkeley and Oakland. (Among them was the home of author Maxine Hong Kingston.) But fires have greatly intensified in the early twenty-first century. Ross Macdonald's noir detective novel, *The Underground Man* (1971), was set against the background of the September 1964 Coyote Fire above Santa Barbara, which was described in the novel as a "fifty-year fire" (p. 691). Such fires are nearly an annual event in that coastal region now.

The reason for this increase, of course, is global warming, the destructive impact of which has been magnified in California by poor zoning and poor forest management. The latter is particularly clear in the Sierra foothills, site of the Butte County town of Paradise. The indigenous people who once lived in Paradise, the Konkows, like woodland Indians everywhere in North America, regularly burned off underbrush, a practice that produced a healthy, open, park-like forest. The policy of federal and state fire-fighting agencies, for decades, has been to suppress all fires whatsoever—though this protocol finally is changing. The degrading of the landscape is apparent even in such jewels of the national park system as Yosemite. Maria Lebrado (Totuya, d. 1931) was the last full-blooded Ahwahneechee, the original inhabitants of the valley, who were forced out by the U.S. Army. Returning to Yosemite after seventy-eight years, she "complained that it was 'dirty' and 'bushy,' for there were trees and shrubs where meadows had been, and undergrowth in the forest …" (Solnit 1994, p. 301).

The fuel of undergrowth, supplemented by millions of conifers killed by beetles flourishing from global warming, has produced, throughout the last decade, firestorms of size and intensity never seen before in California: monster fires that leap freeways and rivers, roar down out of the hills into flatlands and invade towns and suburbs, spread by their own fire-producing lightning strikes, and accompanied by the new and terrifying phenomenon of the fire tornado. The burning of Paradise, whose name is now too obviously ironic, is only one episode of a continuing tragedy.[4]

On November 8, 2018, a fire was sparked by a broken hook falling from a Pacific Gas and Electric power transmission tower east of Paradise. The resulting blaze was fanned by Jarbo winds, the regional version of foehn winds that elsewhere in the state are called Santa Anna or Diablo winds. In three hours, from 6 a.m. to 9 a.m., the fire leaped the west branch of the

Feather River and reached the eastern edge of Paradise. Along the way, it swept over a recreational path called the Ishi Trail. The town of Paradise had seen forest fires before and had developed evacuation plans. Cal Fire, the nation's largest firefighting agency, had a nearby station, went into action immediately, and called for massive reinforcements. Nonetheless, by 1 p.m. the city was enveloped. Eighty-five people would die—some in their homes and many in their cars or on foot while trying to escape.

Paradise had grown slowly through the twentieth century. For its residents, for decades, there was no irony in its name. The town, built in a forest of ponderosa pine, offered reasonably priced homes and a life close to nature. Hiking, hunting, fishing, and other outdoor recreation were available for everyone. The destruction of Paradise exposed the fragility of this life. While we might not read this event as Gothic, it can be seen as part of a collapse of an aspect of California life that was long taken for granted and anticipates the apocalyptic visions we will discuss in later chapters.

Joan Didion, writing of the Santa Anna winds of Southern California and the fires they feed, wrote that "the city burning is Los Angeles's deepest image of itself" (p. 220). The winds remind us, she wrote, "how close to the edge we are" (p. 221). In the new century, it is not just the city but the whole state burning that haunts our imagination.

Endnotes

1   On California as an island, see also Elna Bakker.
2   Murphy, in *Rural Gothic*, traces this pattern though the American literature and film.
3   The 1999 film *Ravenous* (dir. Antonia Bird) also applies the Wendigo myth to fictional Donner-like events in the Sierra. See Murphy's discussion in *California Gothic* pp. 32–39.
4   Journalistic accounts of the Camp Fire are provided by Johnson, and by Gee and Anguiano. The legal consequences for PG & E are recounted by Blunt.

Chapter 2

AMBROSE BIERCE AND SAN FRANCISCO'S GOTHIC FRONTIER

Ghost: The outward and visible sign of an inward fear.
     —Ambrose Bierce, *The Devil's Dictionary*

What city has more or stranger disappearances and assassinations? There have been murders and suicides at all the hotels. Other cities surpass it in age, but none in crime and mystery.
     —Emma F. Dawson, "A Sworn Statement"

In 1845, the village of Yerba Buena had a population of about 300 souls. By 1850, the rechristened San Francisco was the biggest city on the west coast of the United States. San Francisco became rich first from the Gold Rush and then from the Comstock Lode of silver in Nevada. By the 1860s, its wealth as a banking and shipping center brought sophistication in the form of grand buildings, opera, and theater. The city had passed from Cole's "The Savage State" to "The Consummation of Empire" in a single generation.

This growth had come at a cost. The Sierra foothills had been stripped of soil by hydraulic mining, which had flooded the Sacramento Delta and the Bay with silt. The native population of the Central Valley and the Sierra had been largely destroyed. Racial tensions were growing between white settlers and Chinese immigrants. In 1868, a major earthquake destroyed much of the city, underscoring the fragility of the City by the Bay. Such racial and environmental dissonance, suppressed in the narrative of progress, would return in California Gothic.

By the 1860s, San Francisco's young "Bohemians," a group of writers including Bret Harte, Ina Coolbrith, Warren Stoddard, and for a time Mark Twain, had begun what Franklin Walker dubbed (in a 1939 book by that title) "*San Francisco's Literary Frontier.*" The Bohemians, writes Ben Tarnoff, "would bring a fresh spirit to American writing, drawn from the new world being formed in the Far West" (p. 5). Chief among the Bohemians was Bret Harte, who edited *The Golden Era* and then *The Overland Monthly*, a serious publication intended to rival *The Atlantic*, as for a time it did. Yet Harte was not a simple booster of California and the West. He knew its dark side. As a young journalist, he had been driven out of the town of Eureka when he reported honestly on the massacre of a nearby California Indian encampment. His tales of the gold fields were not just humorous or picturesque. Some of them, if not Gothic, could be considered at least "Gothic adjacent." "The Luck of Roaring Camp," for example, begins with miners making bets about the survival of a Native prostitute and the sex of her infant; she dies, and her little boy, though coddled by the miners, dies in a flood. The story is darkly humorous, but very dark indeed. The miners are "barely human" (Tarnoff 2014, p. 157), true savages, made tolerable to readers in San Francisco and New York only by Harte's heavy irony that held them at arm's length. This was the savage state from which San Francisco's consummation of empire had sprung.

With the arrival of Civil War hero Ambrose Bierce, San Francisco's Bohemia acquired a writer who would earn international fame for his Gothic fiction. Bierce wrote ghastly stories about the war, ghost stories, supernatural, and weird tales of all sorts, science fiction, and hoaxes, and was probably the most influential American writer of his era on American Gothic literature in the twentieth century. I will discuss here Bierce's first short story, "The Haunted Valley" (1871), published by Bret Harte in *The Overland Monthly*, and two later stories, "An Inhabitant of Carcosa" (1887) and "The Death of Halpern Frayser" (1893). These two are linked by Bierce's imagined philosopher Hali, who provides an epigraph for each story, but are otherwise quite different. Scholar Sharon Talley considers "The Death of Halpern Frayser" to be Bierce's last significant short story (Talley 2006, p. 170).

Ambrose Bierce was only twenty-nine years old when he published "The Haunted Valley," but this complex story about race and gender, madness, secrets, and partial discoveries is among his best and serves as an introduction to his ironic, highly ambiguous approach to the Gothic.

The tale begins with a description of a rural California road that "dips into a sunless ravine which opens out on either hand in a half-confidential manner, as if it had a secret to impart ... I never used to ride through it without looking first to the one side and then to the other, to see if the time had arrived for the revelation." The paragraph continues in this vein for several sentences and is as dark and tangled as the ravine. We understand that traveling this road is analogous to entering a mystery. In fact, it is like reading a Gothic text, which is gloomy but promises a revelation—the discovery of a secret.

The mystery involves Jo. [sic] Dunfer, a "hairy man" who lives in a "hermaphrodite habitation, half residence and half groggery" with his "Chinaman" servant, Ah Wee, and his employee Gopher, who is a "queer" little white man. When the narrator visits the groggery, Dunfer, drinking heavily, tells him—in a speech that seems compounded of defiant boast, confession, and tall tale—that he murdered Ah Wee because he could not learn to chop down trees in the American way. At this point, Dunfer reacts with horror at the sight of a big black eye peeping through a knothole in the wall. Although the eye is revealed to be that of the queer little man, Gopher, the narrator flees the scene.

As the narrator passes again through the sunless ravine, he turns aside on impulse and encounters another Gothic text, the inscription on Ah Wee's gravestone:

AH WEE—CHINAMAN.
Age unknown. Worked for Jo. Dunfer.
This monument erected by him to keep the Chink's
Memory green. Likewise as a warning to Celestials
Not to take on airs. Devil take 'em!
She Was a Good Egg.

The narrator is astonished by the combination of "impudent candor … brutal anathema … and ludicrous change of sex and sentiment" (p. 121) and concludes that Dunfer must have been mad.

When the narrator returns to the haunted valley four years later, he encounters Gopher, and though Gopher is now partly insane, further revelations ensue. We learn that Dunfer died (apparently from a stroke or heart attack) following the episode of the eye at the knothole; he now lies next to Ah Wee, in an acknowledgment of a long-hidden relationship. We also learn that Dunfer murdered Ah Wee with an axe, not because of her tree-chopping technique but because Dunfer came upon Gopher trying to remove a spider from the sleeping Ah Wee and misinterpreted the scene as an erotic encounter. Gopher also reveals that he had followed Ah Wee from San Francisco and had kept the secret of her gender for years.

Franklin Walker, the great pioneer of California literary studies, sees "The Haunted Valley" as a revenge story. Gopher deliberately frightens Dunfer to death, knowing he will see the eye in the knothole as Ah Wee's ghost. Now he pays for his action with the loss of his own sanity and his terror at meeting Dunfer's ghost. ("Ghost: The outward and visible sign of an inward fear.") But we could read the story as a parable about racism, in which (as Gopher tells us) Dunfer's vile racism battled with his love of Ah Wee, and the conflict "ate 'im up" (p. 126).

Much about the story still baffles the reader, which makes the story seem particularly relevant after some 150 years. A story about a presumably straight man, a cross-dressing woman, and a "queer" little man teases us with unstated possibilities. Though the OED does not confirm that "queer" had any gender implications in 1879, the word may have already carried that edge in the American vernacular. In any case, there are troubling ambiguities concerning both gender and race. Take, for example, the matter of the big black eyes that characterize both Gopher and Ah Wee. Gopher tells us that Ah Wee's eyes were "like mine" (p. 125), and this is how he was able to terrify Dunfer by looking through the knothole. But how can it be that a white man and a Chinese woman had identical eyes? Could Gopher have been a Chinese man passing as white? And what exactly was the relationship between Gopher and Ah Wee? The possibilities are unresolved, and we leave Bierce's haunted valley still waiting for its revelation.

Dumfer had won Ah Wee in a card game in San Francisco's Chinatown, a city within a city that had been swollen by former workers, first from the Sierra gold fields and then from the transcontinental railroad. It continued as a vibrant community, in frequent conflicts with working-class whites (especially Irish immigrants), until it began to wither after the Chinese Exclusion Act of 1882. In rendering Ah Wee's narrative obscure and ambiguous, Bierce anticipates the suppression of this community. The history of this erasure, like that of Indigenous Californians, is part of the great California Uncanny.

A very different story, "An Inhabitant of Carcosa," is the most influential of Bierce's works on later Gothic fiction. The name Carcosa is used by Robert W. Chambers in his *The King in Yellow* stories (1895) as a deliberate act of homage, and through Chambers, Bierce influenced H. P. Lovecraft and the tradition of weird tales in the twentieth century.[1] Narrated by a ghost who discovers that he is a ghost in the story's last sentence, the tale still has power to evoke a chill in the reader. But equally important is the desolate landscape in which the ghost walks.

Like Shelley's poem "Ozymandias" (1818), Bierce's tale depicts a ruined land in which only fragments remain of a once powerful civilization: in Shelley, the broken base of what had been the statue of a mighty king; in Bierce's tale, the few shattered gravestones in an abandoned cemetery all that is left of the rich city of Carcosa. Both works are reminders that great empires (the Roman, the British, and the American) may collapse; in fact, they inevitably do.

America's belief in progress is based on the expectation of limitless growth and expansion. Ruins prove the fragility of that expectation. As Martin Procházka reminds us (pp. 27–40), Americans have long nourished a tradition of religious millenarianism, with the last days predicted in Revelations expected at any moment. But secular thought was also haunted by the collapse of our civilization. The American artist Thomas Cole's

"The Course of Empire" paintings depict a cycle leading at last to ruins. While the empire shown at its height recalls Roman splendor, the "Savage State" from which the empire evolved is represented by Indian tepees, which establishes a parallel to America. In Bierce's west, ruins could already be seen in abandoned mining camps in the Sierra foothills and in the desert, disturbing and dissonant notes in an expanding economy. The literary tradition of the end of days, begun by Mary Shelley's novel *The Last Man* (1826), would become an important—often Gothic—vector in American and California literature, which will be explored in subsequent chapters on disease Gothic and Ecogothic.

"An Inhabitant of Carcosa" begins with a meditation by Bierce's sage Hali about ghosts. "The Death of Halpin Frayser" begins with Hali's description of animated corpses, or "liches," which, though "in life were benign become by death evil altogether" (p. 59).

"The Death of Halpin Frayser" is a self-consciously Gothic tale, with its evil lich, two murders, more than a hint of incest, and a nightmare dream sequence. It is also a detective story, with two lawmen reading the evidence of a crime scene. The detective story and the Gothic tale—the two halves of Poe's fiction—can be joined coherently, as later Noir writers would prove. They are not so integrated here. Bierce's tale has strong elements of self-parody and hoax and rejects the reader's attempt to discover a key that makes sense of the story's several elements, or to resolve its "rascally mystery," as the detectives call it (*Complete Short Stories* 71). It does not anticipate Noir fiction of the twentieth century. Rather, as Cathy N. Davidson argues (p. 113), Bierce anticipates such postmodern writers as Borges.

On one level, the tale seems like a familiar account of a man moving to California to remake his life. He rejects his mother's plea to take her with him, and Bierce hints that he is fleeing an unhealthy relationship with his "Katy." As Sharon Talley observes, "It would be difficult for Bierce to have anticipated Freud with a more obvious description of the Oedipus complex" (p. 162). However, like the flight of Oedipus, Frayser's journey to California has an ironic outcome. After various misadventures in the Pacific, Frayser arrives in the Sonoma Valley only to be murdered on the grave of his mother, who had been killed by her second husband.

Frayser's dream on midsummer's night, the Gothic centerpiece of the tale, repeats the pattern of flight and deadly reunion with the mother. The dream sequence, which has some similarities to Hawthorne's "Young Goodman Brown," and is like it a story of a failed initiation and a nightmare journey into the wilderness. Frayser was lost in the woods when he fell asleep, and he is lost in the woods in his dream. He takes a "road less travelled" (a phrase that must have stuck in the mind of Robert Frost) and finds himself in a forest of bleeding trees, recalling the wood of suicides in Dante's *Inferno*. Frightened and oppressed by a sense of nameless guilt, he tries to record his plight by writing in blood and producing verse in the style of his poet great-grandfather. (Another scene of a doomed man writing in blood, by the way, will be seen in Denis Johnson's *Already Dead*, to be discussed in Chapter 3.) He meets the lich of his mother, is strangled, and "dreamed that he was dead" (p. 66). He is found the next morning by the lawmen, with the notebook of verse beside him.

Bierce's tale is most comprehensible as a symbolic exploration of gender and family pathology. Sharon Talley's Lacanian approach in *The Journal of Men's Studies* convincingly reads the story in cultural as well as individual or family terms. The South had not provided Frayser with an adequate model of masculine character. On a more literal level, the story is an irresolvable puzzle. Was Frayser killed by his mad stepfather? Or was he killed by the vengeful lich of his mother? Whatever way we try to sort the story's dueling explanations, supernatural or realistic, there are bits of the puzzle left on the table. As Cathy N. Davidson summarizes:

> Evidence is there, of course, too much evidence: signs of sin, guilt, expiation, incest, insanity, suicide, self-delusion, revenge. The text taunts at every turn by providing the movement's expected textual solution. The joke lies in the fact that the reader must continually reject these apparent solutions because they do not adequately comprehend the complexities elsewhere in the text. (p. 113)

S. T. Joshi, the leading scholar of the "weird tale," argues, however, that the story is coherent and that Frayser had been living in California with his mother as man and wife (pp. 161–62). This reading is consistent with the strong hints of reciprocal incestuous desire shown early in the tale. Frayser murders his mother and is killed in turn by his mother's "lich."

The problem with this reading is that it does not fit the timeline given to us by the narrator, who states that Frayser has only recently returned to the United States after his years as a Shanghaied sailor and shipwreck victim. Of course, we could say that these adventures seem preposterous, but if we do not have a reliable narrator, we can trust nothing, and the whole tale falls apart in our hands. The uncanny laughter heard at the end of "The Death of Halpin Frayser" may be that of the murderer Branscom or that of the mother's lich. It may be, as W. B. Stein suggests, the "trickster God ... who delights in betraying every aspiration for truth or certitude" (p. 227). But this is just to say that it is Bierce himself, laughing at the absurdity of the world and at us.

Everyone who reads Bierce understands that he was shaped by combat in the American Civil War—in this, he was unique among major American writers. We should remember that Bierce's defining battle was not Gettysburg, with its sweeping vistas and narrative clarity, but rather the chaos of Chickamauga, which was the setting for one of his most disturbing Civil War tales. Chickamauga was a two-day struggle fought in rough wooded terrain where the enemy usually could not be seen, a battle that was lost by the Union on a fluke, had no impact whatsoever on the course of the war, and ended in a night of horror for thousands of men (including Bierce) fleeing for their lives through burning woods—a very Bierce-like event, surely. Chickamauga modeled Bierce's view of a world that ultimately made no sense.

Despite his reputation as an irascible crank who kept a human skull on his desk, Bierce was a mentor and promoter of a small number of young San Francisco writers, including George Sterling (discussed in Chapter 3) and Emma Francis Dawson (1839–1926). Dawson, whom Bierce once called "head and shoulders above any writer on this coast" (Purdy 1926, p. 87), was a thoroughgoing Gothic writer of short stories, which feature haunted houses, curses, vindictive ghosts, and doubles. Her stories often display a strong feminist perspective and acknowledge both the erotic and financial motives of her heroines. "An Itinerant House," the title story of her only collection, has been anthologized and recently discussed by Gothic scholar Dara Downey in terms of Gothic domestic spaces (Downey 2014, *Ghost Stories*, pp. 64–89). In that tale, a boarding house reappears in different locations in San Francisco, bringing its curse to unsuspecting victims. The story is based on the literal wandering of light-weight wooden structures in the city, which were often moved from one location to another (and sometimes still are).

"The Dramatic in My Destiny" is one of the most ambitious of her stories but has received virtually no critical attention, other than in Nina Baym's passing reference to Dawson among other women writers of the American West (p. 80). The story begins with a long, surreal description of an opium dream in which the protagonist, Yorke Rhys, is pursued by a shape-shifting adversary who is revealed as a kind of double. This hallucinatory sequence, which is an impressive piece of writing, anticipates a later episode in which Rhys and a policeman search San Francisco's Chinatown for Si-Ki, a Chinese servant who has murdered Rhys's beloved, Elinor:

> We bent at doorways that barred our path at sudden turns, peered into vile dens that lined the way, and, choking and strangling, climbed above ground, where we scanned the thousands of workmen in the many boot and shoe factories and cigar-works; hunted through the numberless gambling-hells, but could not pass the old watchman, with wrinkled face like a baked apple, sitting on a stool in front of a red curtain (the colour for luck), before he jerked the cord dangling near

him, when bells warned, doors were barred, bolts shot like lightning, door upon door suddenly thrust itself across our path, or a screen slyly slid before us, turning us unaware into another passage. (pp. 115–16)

There are other such nightmarish sequences, all of which may seem to confirm Rhys's description early in the story of the crowds of Chinese as "the rank, poisonous undergrowth in our forest of men" (p. 101).

But these passages do *not* endorse Rhy's prejudices. Contrary to Nina Baym's claim that Dawson presents "San Francisco as a gothic monstrosity, with Chinatown the source and epitome of evil" (p. 80), we should note that it is the narrator, Yorke Rhys, who makes such statements. Rhys is an unreliable narrator, however, and virtually every judgment that he makes early in the story is proved false.[2] He claims to be in control of his own destiny, yet the action of the story shows him blown about by circumstances and his own uncontrollable impulses. He tells his beloved Elinor that he would never take a human life, then kills his best friend in an irrational fit. His beating of Si-Ki with a cane for the crime of touching Elinor's hand while shouting to spectators that it is a matter "Between us two" reveals him to be a bully and a racist, and motivates Si-Ki's revenge. When he at last finds Si-Ki in Chinatown, his antagonist is now a "snow white" leper. Si-Ki's cry, which ends the tale, "Between us two!" confirms him as Rhys's double, as in the opium dream, and implies that his physical corruption is matched by Rhys's moral decay.

Bierce was right in his judgment of Dawson's talent. She was a Gothic writer whose tales show insight into the issues of her time, especially the position of women and the Chinese in California. Dawson's subsequent neglect, poverty, and lonely death in 1926 is another sad story of San Francisco.

Endnotes

1 In a clear case of "anxiety of influence," Lovecraft does not mention "An Inhabitant of Carcosa" in *Supernatural Horror in Literature* (1927), though he praises other stories by Bierce. I am indebted to my colleague, Faye Ringel, for pointing this out to me.

2 Dawson uses the same technique in "The Second Card Wins," in which "the lovely Mrs. Claire" boasts of her ability "to read people at a glance," but the unfolding action reveals that she understands nothing about anything.

Chapter 3

LOST COASTS

This coast, crying out for tragedy like all beautiful places ...
—Robinson Jeffers, "Apology for Bad Dreams"

Whatever we make here, whatever find, We cannot leave behind.
—Josephine Miles, "After This, Sea"

California's bohemians, beats, or hippies—as the name has changed over the decades—have sought refuge, enlightenment, or community among the forests and surf of the central and north coasts since the early twentieth century. This chapter follows these dreamers from the Carmel colony and the rugged Big Sur to the remote area known as the Lost Coast. Their stories were shaped into Gothic narratives by writers as diverse as John Steinbeck, Thomas Pynchon, Denis Johnson, and Kem Nunn.

Et in Arcadia Ego

The Carmel artist colony produced few works of Gothic literature, if we discount the weird longer poems of George Sterling, which I consider to be dreadful. But the history of this tribe is itself a Gothic story and is the prototype of many stories of wrecked illusions in the coastal California landscape.

The community began as an outpost of the vigorous bohemian culture of San Francisco. The ideas of John Muir were in the air, and the great San Francisco earthquake of 1906 was a further incentive to escape the metropolis. The first bohemian pioneers in Carmel built cabins in the idiom of the emerging Bay Area regional tradition, developed by architects like A. Page Brown and Bernard Maybeck, that stressed a connection with the landscape and use of local materials, as described by architectural historians Freudenheim and Sussman. The poet George Sterling's cabin featured a 30 by 18-foot living room finished in oiled redwood and a massive fireplace and chimney built of chalk rock he hauled himself from the Carmel Valley. The photographer Arnold Genthe built a cabin with a huge combination studio and living room, with massive roof beams supported by redwood trunks with the bark left on.

Never to be upstaged in the back-to-nature department, Mary Austin, already celebrated for *The Land of Little Rain* (1903), built a treehouse, which she called a wik-i-up, as a writer's studio, and often could be glimpsed walking through the forest dressed in flowing Grecian robes, or the fringed and beaded dress of an Indian princess.

At the center of the Carmelites, master of their revels, was George Sterling (Fig. 3.1). Now nearly forgotten, Sterling once seemed the most promising poet of the Pacific Coast. Handsome, charismatic, and athletic, Sterling swam in the surf and endlessly hiked and hunted in Big Sur and the Santa Lucias. He and a core of his friends, including Genthe, the painter Xavier Martinez, the athlete and story writer Jimmy Hopper, the poet Nora May French, and, to a lesser extent, Mary Austin, created the distinctive culture of the Carmel bohemians, a culture mingling physical fitness, trendy European philosophy, Eastern mysticism and Native American religion, relaxed sexual mores,

Figure 3.1 George Sterling.

nude sunbathing, wine, and recreational drugs that would not have been out of place in Berkeley in the 1960s. Yet Sterling's closest literary friends, Jack London and Ambrose Bierce, though they often visited Carmel, ultimately decided not to build cabins among the Carmel redwoods. Both sensed that something was wrong in this Eden.

In London's novel *The Valley of the Moon*, his protagonists, Billy and his wife Saxon, leave the brutal working-class world of Oakland, determined to find a better life. They want to learn what went wrong with the California dream and find a way to live in harmony with the landscape. This vision—the place and the life—they call "the valley of the moon." When they reach Carmel, they believe that they have found it.

Billy and Saxon are welcomed by the artists and writers. Billy, who has been a professional boxer, soon will be swimming in the surf, rock climbing, and running races on the beach with the athletic Carmel men. He helps them in the dangerous harvesting of abalone from the rocks, and the Carmelites teach Billy and Saxon the central ritual of their clan, the pounding of abalone while chanting the endless verses of their song:

> Oh! some folks boast of quail on toast,
>   Because they think it's tony;
> But I'm content to own my rent
>   And live on abalone.
>   …
>
> Oh! some like ham and some like lamb,
>   And some like macaroni;
> But bring me in a pail of gin
>   And a tub of abalone. (II, pp. 386–87)

Billy and Saxon are initiated into the Tribe of Abalone Eaters. Saxon even contributes a verse to the abalone-pounding song. Fascinated by the freedom of the Abalone Eaters and especially by the personality of their leader, Mark Hall (Hall Mark, Sterling), Billy, and Saxon spent the winter in this apparent utopia.

But in calling them the Tribe of Abalone Eaters, recalling Tennyson's "mild-eyed, melancholy Lotos-eaters" (*Works* 51), London exposes the underlying entropy and nihilism at the core of their lives, despite the apparent "childlike joy" (II, p. 393) of their games. Saxon "could never comprehend … the pessimism that so often cropped up" (II, p. 408), and "was oppressed by these sad children of art. It was inconceivable that they, of all people, should be so forlorn" (II, p. 409). And so, after their winter with the Abalone Eaters, Billy and Saxon shouldered their packs and set out again in search of their Valley of the Moon, which was not to be found in Carmel after all.

In his novel, London attributes the sadness of the Carmel group in part to destructive ideas, especially those of Nietzsche. But there were also specific personality traits and events that sent ripples through the group, and not all had been revealed at the time of *The Valley of the Moon*.

A nearly forgotten early novel by Mary Austin, *Outland* (1910), is a glimpse into the ethos of the abalone eaters. *Outland* was first published in England under the pseudonym Gordon Stairs. Austin did not reissue it in the United States under her own name until 1919. Perhaps this nearly furtive publication was Austin's attempt to distance herself and to provide a protective cloak over her Carmel friends, so that it would not be read as the *roman à clef* we now understand it to be. *Outland* was, in fact, a collective fantasy of the abalone eaters. In a much later article in *The Overland Monthly*, Austin describes the origin of the book in conversations among the group in Carmel ("A Poet," p. 331, 351), while in her preface to the 1919 Boni and Liveright edition, she states that the narrative was jointly written by her and George Sterling. While these memories may not be entirely consistent, they do indicate that the roots of the story were deep in the Carmel experience.

Outland tells how two visitors to a coastal community wander into nearby woods and discover a tribe of people who live there in perpetual hiding from the "house people," as they call our culture. These secret forest dwellers recall faeries and elves of European lore, as well as Peter Pan's Lost Boys and perhaps Robin Hood's band. Of course they also recall the Esselen people who once inhabited the Carmel Valley and Big Sur—and it is noteworthy that *Outland* was published the year *before* the 1911 appearance of Ishi in Oroville, whose Yahi group had been living for years just such a life of hiding in the Sierra foothills.

While staying among these elf-Indians, Mona, the narrator (clearly based on Austin), and her companion Herman (i.e., Her Man) are partially accepted by the Outliers and participate with them in a war fought with another secret tribe, the Far Folk. Among the Outliers there are recognizable embodiments of the Carmel group: among them, most importantly, there is a wise woman with prophetic powers (also based on Austin, of course), Ravenutzi, a charismatic and handsome hostage from the Far Folk, representing George Sterling, a tall, dark-haired Far Folk woman, in whom recognize Carrie Sterling, George's wife, while the blonde and lovely Zirriloë, with whom all the men fall in love, is Nora May French. The leader of the Outliers may represent Jack London.

The plot of *Outland* involves a war between the Outliers and the Far Folk over a disputed treasure. At the end of the narrative, the characters representing Sterling, Carrie Sterling, and Nora May French are dead—as, in reality, Carrie and Nora May already were.

Figure 3.2 Nora May French.

Nora May French (1881–1907, Fig. 3.2) was the dark princess of the Carmel tribe. One of her sayings had been written on the wall of San Francisco's bohemian hangout, Coppa's Restaurant: "I fancy that all sensible people ultimately will be damned" (Walker 1973, *Seacoast*, p. 33). French was beautiful, blonde, and a talented poet. Though she grew up in Southern California in relative poverty, she was the grand-niece of Henry Wells, founder of Wells-Fargo and American Express. Her profound bouts of melancholy might lead today to a diagnosis of bipolar disorder, but, truly, her many unhappy love affairs, some of which led to abortions, would justify deep depression. Like the later Sylvia Plath, she wrote about death's appeal: "Always the outer hall is very still, /And on my face a pleasant wind and clear/Blows straitly from the narrow gate of Death" (Poems p. 75). Sensing what was coming, Mary Austin left Carmel because, as she later wrote, she did not want to see Nora French die (*Woman* p. 256). On November 7, 1907, while staying at the Sterling house, she took cyanide.[1] She was twenty-six years old. The Abalone Eaters scattered her ashes in Carmel Bay and would commemorate the anniversary of her death for years. George Sterling would write poems inspired by Nora May for the rest of his life. (See, for example, "The Ashes in the Sea" [p. 169].)

French's suicide changed the culture of the Carmel colony. While not exactly turning it into a death cult, French made suicide an option, if not a goal, within its darkening, contracting circle. The next to follow was Carrie Sterling, George's now-estranged wife, who also took cyanide the following year. George Sterling lived until 1926, long enough to acknowledge his failure to achieve the fame that everyone once predicted for him and to have welcomed the Carmel successor who would achieve this fame, Robinson Jeffers. Sterling died in his room in the Bohemian Club in San Francisco in the style of Nora May, having finally taken the cyanide that, according to Franklin Walker, he had carried with him for years. Among his effects were the charred fragments of a poem he was writing about darkness and a love poem written to him by Nora May (Walker 1973, p. 121; Prendergast 2021, p. 285).

In *The Valley of the Moon*, Carmel's Lotos Land was a trap for London's characters Billy and Saxon, as the Darwinian sink of Oakland had been before. They continue their odyssey, wandering the California landscape, searching for their Valley of the Moon. Eventually they reach a landscape that draws this response from Saxon: "I know I've never been here before … But it's all so familiar! So I must have dreamed it. —And there's madroños!—a whole grove! And Manzanita! Why, I feel as if I was coming home" (II, p. 479). Later they learn that the valley's name, Sonoma, means in the language of its original Miwok and Pomo inhabitants, The Valley of the Moon.

Billy and Saxon's discovery of their home place mirrors Jack London's own discovery of land near Glen Ellen in the Sonoma Valley that became his Beauty Ranch, which he spent the rest of his life transforming into a model of sustainable use. However, in a later novel set in the same valley on a similar ranch, *The Little Lady of the Big House* (1915), the hero commits suicide, as did the hero of his earlier autobiographical novel, *Martin Eden* (1909). Jack London scholars are not convinced that London's own death in 1916 was a suicide, and neither am I, but his old friend George Sterling believed that it was. Though London continued to grow and innovate as a writer, his last few years were filled with illness and disappointment. He planned a vast house in the Bay Area regional tradition that also echoed, on a grand scale, the cabins of his friends in Carmel.[2] Its great redwood pillars, like those of Arnold Genthe's lodge, retained their natural bark. Such a house, built of redwood and local stone, might last for hundreds of years. It burned down the night before Jack and Charmian were to occupy it. The melancholy ruins of Wolf House (Fig. 3.3), their lost home, is one of California's true Gothic places.

Figure 3.3 Ruins of Jack London's Wolf House.

Blood Rites

John Steinbeck's only Gothic novel, *To a God Unknown* (1933), is set in the San Antonio River Valley, just over the Santa Lucia range behind Big Sur, though one key episode occurs on the Carmel headlands. Steinbeck's novel has a tenuous but real connection with Sterling and his abalone eaters through the intermediary figure of Robinson Jeffers.

George Sterling had faded from the Carmel scene for a time, leaving for New York in 1914. This was, by chance, the year that Robinson Jeffers arrived in Carmel with his wife Una. Franklin Walker records that Jeffers and Una were walking in the woods near Carmel when they came upon a glade decorated by Sterling with cattle skulls, as if the site of a primitive ritual. However, Sterling and the Jeffers were not to meet for another decade, and were friends for the last two years of the older poet's life. Sterling even tried to teach Jeffers to dive for abalone, though Jeffers did not enjoy shellfish.

High in his Tor House, which he had built of native stone, Jeffers faced west from California's shores toward Asia and meditated on his position at the edge of western migration and, perhaps, in another sense, at the end of western civilization. His philosophy of "Inhumanism" rejects what he considered the human self-regard of the world's major religions and stresses a view of nature as "only matter and energy; no spirit or soul, no immortal realms" (Brophy 1975, p. 10). There is beauty and divinity in the vast and terrible cycles of nature. In poems like "The Roan Stallion" and "Tamar," the characters are mythic and perform the cycles of death and rebirth.

Jeffers himself may be represented by a hermit met by Joseph Wayne (the protagonist of *To a God Unknown*) and his brother when they make an excursion to the coast. The hermit lives in a house overlooking the sea and claims that at day's end he is "the last man in the western world to see the sun" (p. 143). The hermit sacrifices an animal on a stone altar each evening in a ceremony that sanctifies the passing of the day. While Jeffers never would have harmed an animal, such blood rituals are common in his verse, and, in a sense, his poems themselves are acts of sacrifice, as he explained in "An Apology for Bad Dreams":

> Better invent than suffer: imagine victims
> Lest your own flesh be chosen the agonist, or you
> Martyr some creature to the beauty of the place.... (p. 11)

In Steinbeck's novel, the idea of blood sacrifice, thus introduced, pulls us toward the story's uncanny but inevitable conclusion.

Joseph Wayne brings his extended family from New England to the valley and falls in love with the California landscape. He wants to possess it spiritually and physically and, in a somewhat absurd scene, even attempts to have sex with it. At first, the land seems to welcome the Waynes and bring an abundant harvest. A fiesta at the center of the novel is a harvest festival in which the several religious traditions of the valley are observed: the priest from the nearby mission offers prayers, and the Mexican villagers and ranch hands dance, while indigenous Indians (they would have been Xolons) stamp and shuffle around in a circle. Burton, Joseph's puritanical brother, prays apart from these heathenish rituals.

Of the various religions present, none except the largely invisible indigenous beliefs adequately express the landscape. Nor does Joseph's gentle mysticism, which seems compounded of ideas from Emerson and Swedenborg. The valley that has appeared to provide a welcoming home turns uncanny when Joseph discovers a mysterious glade:

> In the center of the clearing stood a rock as big as a house, mysterious and huge ... The edifice was something like an altar that had melted and run down over itself. In one side of the rock there was a small black cave fringed with five-fingered ferns, and from the cave a little stream flowed silently and crossed the glade and disappeared into the tangled brush that edged the clearing. Beside the stream a great black bull was lying, his front legs folded under him.... (p. 29)

With its obvious fertility symbols, the glade expresses the vitality of the land. Elizabeth, Joseph's wife, finds the glade "evil" (p. 100), while Joseph finds "strength and sweetness" (p. 119) in the place. It is both good and evil, and neither, representing the vast forces of nature that, as in Jeffers' poetry, are outside and beyond comfortable human belief. Ultimately the glade will claim the lives of both Elizabeth and Joseph. Elizabeth slips and falls while trying to climb the rock, and Joseph makes of himself a blood sacrifice upon its altar, thus ending a brutal drought. Earlier, Joseph's sister-in-law, the wise woman or good witch Rama, called Joseph a "godling." At the end, Joseph becomes a kind of puppet, like a Jeffers character, expressing the forces of nature. "I am the land ... and I am the rain," Joseph thinks as his blood drains over the altar. "The grass will grow out of me in a little while" (p. 179). And so it rains, and the land is restored.

The Matter of the Sixties

The art colony of Carmel was ultimately displaced by the gentrifying development that has made the town today a wealthy enclave with artistic pretentions. (It says much about the current ambiance that there is a Thomas Kincade gallery in Carmel, as well as an annual poodle show.) By the 1930s, the real bohemians were moving south along Highway 1 into Big

Sur and building simple cabins and studios in the mountains and canyons. Among them was Henry Miller, whose memoir *Big Sur and the Oranges of Hieronymus Bosch* (1957) describes his life there in the 1940s and 50s. (He would remain in Big Sur until 1963).

Miller's book is filled with episodes of guests who were unexpected and intrusive or who outstayed their welcome, disrupting his life as a writer and painter. One guest who would have been welcome, at least for a time, was Jack Kerouac. His failure to keep an appointment with Miller, whose work and life had been important to Kerouac, is evidence of Kerouac's mental disintegration at the time.

Kerouac's autobiographical novel about his brief stay in Lawrence Ferlinghetti's cabin, *Big Sur*, is not considered Gothic, but it is filled with Gothic images, from his arrival at night near the Bixby Bridge to his walk through the darkness, which anticipates his later alcoholic collapse. While his stay in the cabin was intended to serve as a wholesome retreat, Kerouac soon brought others to the cabin, including Neal Cassady's San Francisco girlfriend, and began the binge drinking that led to a period of madness. The reader is likely to feel, rather than the Gothic uncanny, pity and disgust at Kerouac's waste of his energy and talent.

Kerouac was bemused and sometimes appalled by his fame as the "king of the beats." Nonetheless, the Kerouac of *On the Road* (1957), *The Subterraneans* (1958) and *The Dharma Bums* (1958), would serve as models for the counterculture that followed in the 1960s. As F. Scott Fitzgerald said, a generation takes its ideas "from the madmen and the outlaws of the generation before" (p. 155).

The story of the Sixties and what happened to its illusions—what might be called the Matter of the Sixties—is far reaching. Our concern here is with novels set in the woodlands and coastal hills of Northern California, in which the aftermath of that era was played out through the following decades in Gothic terms. We will look briefly at Thomas Pynchon's postmodern comic Gothic (for so I see it) *Vineland* (1990) and then at two under-appreciated true Gothics, Denis Johnson's *Already Dead: A California Gothic* (1997) and Kem Nunn's *The Dogs of Winter* (1997), all having action in the northern coastal regions that include the legendary "Lost Coast," the most remote and inaccessible region in the state. In each case, however, the author has tinkered with the geography, so that the settings often "are not down on any map," as Melville might have said, because "true places never are" (p. 852).

Vineland is full of Gothic tropes and types, including a kind of zombie, the Thanatoids, who are but another community among the aging hippies in the north-coast redwoods.

The present of Pynchon's *Vineland* is in the mid-eighties, but dips back to the sixties, and glances back even further, and constitutes a history of the disillusionment not only of sixties idealism but of the longer history of American progressivism. The grandparents of Prairie Wheeler, the novel's heroine, were labor organizers in the 1930s and victims of the "red scare" in the 1950s. Prairie's mother, Frenesi Gates, was a student radical in the 1960s, who has disappeared. The search for Prairie's mother, in a detective-style plot typical of Pynchon, leads to the discovery of the narrative's "original sin," Frenesi's betrayal of her film-collective colleagues to a federal prosecutor, Brock Vond, which led to the death of Weed Atman. This single act of betrayal is a stand-in for the failure of the idealism of a generation, of its co-opting by the forces of government, the war on drugs, and the powers of money and the media. Nonetheless, the novel is a kind of comedy, not only because of Pynchon's satirical humor but also because it ends in reconciliation and the villain, Brock Vond, being carried away to Yurok hell in a tow truck.

Already Dead and The *Dogs of Winter* share with *Vineland* a Lost Coast setting and a present that is filled with melancholy echoes of sixties idealism. In the coastal redwoods, witchcraft is practiced and marijuana is harvested. Indigenous people are present, as ghosts or (in *The Dogs of Winter*) a living presence.

The Carmel artists were energized by the great changes of the Progressive Era, which was the true beginning of the twentieth century in America. Decades later, another period of upheaval again sent young Californians into the woods and deserts in search of a new life. Although Denis Johnson's *Already Dead* is set in the 1990s, it belongs on the shelf of books about the sixties in California and their collapse: the "Matter of the Sixties." In the nineties, on the remote Lost Coast of Northern California, the "Haight-Ashbury dialect flourishes unevolved" (p. 37). Early in the novel, Nelson Fairchild, Jr. (whom the reader will finally understand to be the novel's protagonist), drives past redwoods that

> ... shade and hide the twisted dregs of the old communes—once the best, the finest people, lured here by the piping of a lovely song and then held by drugs or religion, isolated minds bending around tightly to feed on themselves.
>
> Those ghostly hippies, do you think I feel sorry for them? No. They came here and did what they dreamed of. The lovely song becomes a shape, and strides forth. (pp. 28–29)

The novel reveals the shapes that remain in and emerge from the forest, which now conceals the trailers and shacks of old hippies and their recent recruits, a few fine homes, like that of Fairchild, and the secret marijuana plots, like Fairchild's, that drive the local underground economy.

Strangely, the basic plot of *Already Dead* is drawn from another's work, "Poem Noir" by Bill Knott. As in a typical noir story, the poem's protagonist, motivated by greed or lust, commits a crime that sets in motion a cascading series of unintended consequences. Here, Fairchild is fearful that his father will disinherit him in favor of his estranged wife, costing him his home among the redwoods, and he contracts with a stranger to murder her. The result, however, will be his own death, his father's, and his brother's, while the stranger will marry the widow, who now owns a house and forest.

To this core plot, however, Johnson adds many characters, complications, and layers of meaning. A recurring juggler and magician called the Tregetour, in fact, seems a mask for the author himself, spinning the complexities of this fragmented narrative. There is a character called Frankenstein, a witch, various drug dealers and users, and two hitmen called the pig hunters, who are part of an entirely separate conspiracy to kill Fairchild. The reader, lacking the roadmap of Knott's poem, struggles to discover even which of the characters might be the protagonist, first believing it to be Carl Van Ness, the character we meet in the opening pages, who is driving to the Lost Coast on a spiritual quest. The ambiguity is useful since Van Ness, the murderer, becomes Fairchild's alter-ego, his Mr. Hyde. Later, in a séance, Yvonne the Witch will warn Fairchild that he has an evil double who is trying to destroy him. Every character we meet is, in Fairchild's words, an isolated mind bending around tightly to feed on itself, a collection of psychotics, sociopaths, and druggies—some of whom, however, are quite funny. The reader searches in vain for a character representing a moral center. Perhaps Meadows, the surfer saint and war hero, who is Fairchild's partner in the marijuana business; or John Navarro, the sheriff's deputy and former LAPD officer, who brings a cynical LA noir sensibility to the novel; but in each case we are blindsided and repelled by the character's actions, as when Navarro rapes Yvonne, or Meadows slaughters a beautiful dog, or later kills the pig hunters and roasts and eats their hearts.

The general nastiness of the several plots among the redwoods is summed up by the Austrian hippy Melissa, Fairchild's girlfriend (and Frankenstein's): "It's supposed to be a place of healing. I don't know what happened. Somebody did something very dark" (p. 338).

Indeed, while the events of *Already Dead* might be explained by the noir motives of lust and greed, many characters are convinced that supernatural forces have been loosed. Bill Fairchild (Nelson's brother) has seen a demon named Miran, and this demon speaks through Yvonne, urging Navarro to rape her. Perhaps a demon entered Van's body when he died in the pond. (Frankenstein believes this.) Perhaps Nelson's wife really died and is a demon too. And there are ghosts as well, which are seen by Fairchild when he is wounded by the pig hunters and dying in the woods, trying to write his last journal entries in his own blood: ghosts of the recently killed, including his father, ghosts of pioneers, and finally, the ghosts of the Pomo Indians who once held the land.

In the novel's last scene, Van and Nelson's widows (or the demons who inhabit their bodies) are married in a Wiccan ceremony on Halloween. Officer John Navarro watches from a distance and notes that Yvonne seems terrified. Navarro will resign from the sheriff's department later that day, the tough Los Angeles cop realizing that he is outclassed by the evil among these haunted redwoods.

The aging hippies of the Lost Coast, like the Abalone eaters, failed in their attempt to reenter Eden. This is a quest and a failure that have followed Americans across the continent. Ambrose Bierce said, with considerable insight, that he would not move to Carmel because he was "warned by Hawthorne and Brook Farm" (Walker 1973, *Seacoast* p. 96). Hawthorne's imaginative retelling of the Brook Farm story in *The Blithedale Romance* (1852) accurately forecasts the fate of later dreamers. The old life and the old self cannot be left behind. Another glossing of this truth can be found in a Buddhist fable retold early in *Already Dead*:

> A wanderer rests beneath a tree, and wishes for food and drink, and it miraculously appears, since this is a magic wishing tree. He wishes for a home, and it appears, then for a wife. After making love to the beautiful woman, he starts to drift off to sleep, "and suddenly wondered with alarm if these wishes weren't being granted, perhaps, by some sort of devil. Sure enough, a terrifying devil, red as anger, huge and stinking of rot, appeared before him. And right in front of his wife and his gorgeous home, the monster tore him to pieces and ate him. (p. 21)

What we build here, whatever find, unfortunately, is only ourselves.

Surf Gothic and the Lost Coast

Kem Nunn's *The Dogs of Winter*, a surfing drama set on an imaginatively adjusted Northern California coast, recalls the roots of American Gothic, especially tales of Indian warfare (as in C. B. Brown's *Edgar Huntly*) and Indian captivity narratives. Nunn even labels Kenda Harmon's abduction and rape by three vengeful Hupa men "The Captive's Tale." Kendra's escape may be aided by her practice of witchcraft.

The plot of *The Dogs of Winter* is driven by the Ahab-like aging surfer, Drew Harmon (Kendra's husband), who intends to locate a site of legendary giant waves called Heart Attacks and ride them with a magic board he has crafted of balsa and redwood: "You paddle out on that ... the spirits will smile on you" (p. 86). On his quest for Heart Attacks, Harmon drags Fletcher, a once-celebrated surfing photographer, and two young surfing champions, sent by a magazine to be photographed with Harmon at Heart Attacks. The narrative is filled with Gothic tropes, including witchcraft—not only that practiced by Kendra, but the dark magic practiced by Hupa *hee-dee* men and shaman women who practice healing magic. A Hupa word, as understood by Travis McCade, who heads a local Indian Development Council, is *Oo-ma-ha*, which means "something like 'beware,' but carried with it a dimension of time. Beware now, here and now, of this place, of this thing." Travis believes that "the presence of Kendra Harmon called forth that word as well" (p. 39).

Within this ominous zone, other Gothic elements are visible. There is a dark secret involving the murder of Harmon's girlfriend, Amanda, that will surface late in the story. Characters are in several ways doubles: Drew and Fletcher, both seeking to redeem their past fame in a transcendent moment; Fletcher and Travis, with failed marriages and stalled careers, both infatuated with Kendra; and, especially, Amanda and Kendra, who has taken to wearing the clothing of her dead predecessor and styling her hair in the same fashion.

Harmon lives at a river's mouth, in a trailer that once belonged to Amanda. The river is at this point Yurok territory, but Harmon cares nothing for the "old ways" or rights of Indigenous people. The only tribe he cares about is the tribe of surfers, who have their own legends and lore. Thus, it is an insult to the local people when he hires a Hupa boy to take Fletcher into the surf to photograph the riding of the big waves. The Hupas have upriver fishing rights but are not allowed at the river's mouth. The death of the Hupa boy, David Little, when his inadequate boat capsizes in the surf is the turning point of the narrative, for it will bring, a night later, the revenge attack of Hupa men.

Drew Harmon is killed a few days later, after hiking along the coast, through Indigenous land, to a place called "Humaliwu, the place of the big water, the place where the legends die" (p. 43), which he believes to be the true Heart Attacks. In the end, he achieves transcendence, for he is shot by a vengeful Hupa man in the act of surfing a monster wave, perhaps the greatest wave ever ridden. Trailing blood, he is taken by a great white shark. Harmon never faces charges for the death of Amanda and instead earns a place in the lore of his own tribe. Surfers later gather at the site of his death to celebrate Harmon, beneath a bluff where there is an Indigenous cemetery.

Kendra survives her captivity narrative by leading her captor into a trap and taking him to a cabin in the woods where a shaman woman once lived, who might remove the curse she has placed upon him. But, as Kendra knows, the shaman is now dead, and the cabin is occupied by violent marijuana growers. The appearance of an armed man near their cabin provokes a gun battle in which everyone but Kenda is killed. Later, wandering along a road, Kenda is picked up by a Native woman who must be a healing shaman and taken to a battered women's shelter in Redding—a real California city—since Kenda has escaped Nunn's reimagined Gothic Lost Coast.

For Fletcher, the ending is more complex and is an appropriate place to end this chapter. He also achieves transcendence by taking a perfect photograph of one of the young surfing champions in the curl of a big wave at the river's mouth, just before David Little is drowned. The photo makes the cover of a surfing magazine, becomes a poster hung on the walls of surfers around the world, and restores his lost fame as a photographer. However, he abandons his career for something unexpected.

Although Fletcher was not really at fault for David Little's death, he accepts responsibility for it. With the aid of Travis, he contacts Little's impoverished family and arranges to pay them compensation for the boy's death, which is in keeping with Hupa custom. The monthly stipend he pays, we are led to understand, comes from the marijuana crop of the dead growers, which he learned about from Kendra. He buys a cabin near the Oregon border and becomes nearly invisible, though he is known by the locals. "It was said by them that he had made recompense in accordance with the old ways, and they let him be, though some thought him a little strange as he was also known to walk the river alone at night" (p. 361).

Fletcher has become, in other words, an Outlander, like those imagined by Mary Austin.

Though he has not become Native—no *wagay* truly can—he has become as close as anyone to the goal sought by so many California Bohemians since the time George Sterling roamed the woods at Big Sur.

Endnotes

1   Catherine Prendergast's recent meticulously researched book about George Sterling, Carrie Sterling, and Norah May French presents strong, though not conclusive, evidence that Carrie was pregnant with Sterling's child. See *The Gilded Edge* (New York: Dutton, 2021), pp. 187–89.

2   London worked with architect Albert Farr.

Chapter 4

DISEASE, PANDEMICS, AND THE MONSTROUS

It occurred to me that there was no difference between men, in intelligence or race, so profound as the difference between the sick and the well.

—F. Scott Fitzgerald, *The Great Gatsby*

At that time Tod knew very little about them except that they had come to California to die.

—Nathanael West, "The Day of the Locust"

California has long been associated with sunshine and healthy outdoor living. Yet there is an alternative, a dark side, in the realm of California Gothic: California as the site of disease: diseases like tuberculosis (TB) and the secret, shameful syphilis, or AIDs, or imagined diseases that might destroy civilization, perhaps by turning humanity into zombies or vampires. Illness, as Susan Sontag has schooled us, can be a metaphor and can reveal our anxieties about ourselves, our society, and our belief in progress. Here, as in other ways, California has been the bleeding edge of American culture at large. This chapter is a quick trip through a statue gallery, or pest house, of more than a century of California Disease Gothic.

Not long after the Gold Rush had nearly wrecked California's foothills and waterways through hydraulic mining and miners and settlers had massacred most of the state's interior native population, visitors and residents began to promote its wholesome climate. John Muir wrote of hiking and mountaineering in the Sierra as physically and spiritually healing—a faith still celebrated by the Sierra Club. The dry Mediterranean climate of Southern California might heal lung disease. Charles Fletcher Loomis, for example, walked from Ohio to Los Angeles in 1884 seeking to cure his TB and stayed to edit the magazine *Land of Sunshine* (later *Out West*) and promote California as a destination of health and prosperity.

People came. Probably *Health* should be inserted into the title of Claire Faye Watkins's novel, *Gold Fame Citrus*, as a reason for the state's boom.

And there was good reason to flee the cities of the East and Europe, which were, in fact, cesspools of disease. According to Lyra Kilston,

> The nineteenth century witnessed a grim march of epidemic diseases without remedy. Tuberculosis was the leading cause of death in Europe and in the United States where an estimated 70 to 90 percent of the urban population was infected and eight in ten of those who ultimately contracted the disease died …. (p. 17)

Thus the paradox that the land of sunshine and health, especially the Southland, was filling up with sick and dying. Kevin Starr notes that:

> Starting in the late 1870s … influxes of consumptive health seekers poured into Southern California in search of recovery... Many, however, lost their struggle for health and succumbed, and this drama of hope and defeat conferred upon Southern California a certain interplay of healthfulness and morbidity that in various forms, including the hard-boiled detective story and the film noir, would persist until the mid-twentieth century. (*California* 147)

I note, for example, that Raymond Chandler's *The Big Sleep* (1939), an important early landmark in noir detective fiction, begins in the greenhouse of the dying General Sternwood, where "plants filled the place, a forest of them, with nasty meaty leaves and stalks like the newly washed fingers of dead men. They smelled as overpowering as boiling alcohol under a blanket" (p. 6).

As Chandler's description indicates, Gothic imagery is easily associated with disease. Susan Sontag observes that "The most terrifying illnesses are those perceived not just as lethal but as dehumanizing, literally so" (p. 126), as illustrated by rabies, syphilis, and AIDS (p. 129).

In transforming the familiar self into something else, such diseases are inherently *uncanny*. Gothic tropes have long represented the enduring epidemics of TB and syphilis. Both are associated with vampires, as Faye Ringel has shown with TB, and Elaine Showalter with syphilis. Yet the diseases have quite different effects. TB was universally recognized and carried with it a little stigma or guilt. Syphilis, as sexually transmitted, was shameful, a forbidden topic, and for that reason, it built an unspoken fear that each sex had of the other, as Showalter has explored in brilliant detail.

Syphilis Gothic

In the late nineteenth century, Henrik Ibsen, in his play *Ghosts* (1881), may have been the only major writer to confront syphilis directly. The play was, of course, widely denounced and censored. Other novelists and playwrights, as Showalter discusses, such as Wilde, Hardy, and Stevenson, often use imagery suggestive of syphilis without explicitly describing or naming it. Even Émile Zola, though no stranger to censorship, seems to blink in the matter of venereal disease. He has the eponymous heroine of his novel *Nana* (1877) die of smallpox, not syphilis (the great pox), to which her career as a "grand horizontal" must surely have exposed her.

The Californian Frank Norris (who for a time signed himself "The Boy-Zola") was probably the first American writer to present a protagonist suffering from syphilis in his early novel *Vandover and the Brute* (1914). Norris even mentions congenital syphilis, which had brought outrage upon Ibsen, as in this rant from his protagonist, Vandover, to his drinking friends about the Victorian double standard:

> To a large extent I really believe that it's the women's fault that the men are what they are. If they demanded a higher moral standard the men would come up to it; they encourage a man to go to the devil and then—when he's rotten with disease and ruins his wife and has children—what is it—*'spotted toads'*—then there's a great cry raised against the men, and women write books and all, when half the time the woman has only encouraged him to be what he is. (p. 99)

Vandover's opinions are rubbish, of course, but the passage shows Norris's knowledge of the late nineteenth-century feminist debates about sexually transmitted disease discussed by Elaine Showalter. It is also dramatically ironic, since Vandover, unknowingly, has already contracted syphilis.

Vandover and the Brute is a rake's progress that follows its artist-hero's decline from upper middle-class status to, literally, the gutter—a descent that allows Norris to present a detailed cross-section of San Francisco's social classes and especially of the lives of its young men. Vandover's descent could be seen in moralistic terms, as he fails again and again to resist temptation and fails to live up to the Teddy Roosevelt-style muscular Christianity that is the era's default standard of successful masculinity. The turning point of the novel is Vandover's impregnation of Ida Wade, which leads to her suicide and Vandover's expulsion from genteel society. When his father dies and he is rejected by his upper-class fiancée, Turner Ravis, the last hooks restraining his descent are broken. Vandover is cheated of a part of his inheritance by a former friend, and he enters the long, slow slide, marked by compulsive gambling and alcoholism, that will lead to his destruction.

Yet a moralistic, *Ten-Nights-in-a Barroom* reading of the novel would ignore Norris's view of the universe as controlled by impersonal forces, not moral choices. The force that destroys Vandover is disease. We do not know when Vandover was infected: perhaps through his first encounter with a prostitute while a student at Harvard, perhaps by Flossie, a frequent visitor to the private rooms in the restaurants Vandover frequents with his friends, or at the tenderloin brothels that are mentioned but not described. But clearly, Vandover's degeneration is the result of his encroaching "general paralysis of the insane," which had been correctly identified in the Victorian period as a final state of syphilis, when the disease attacks the nervous system. A passage from a book by a physician of the time, Dr. Henry Maudsley (quoted by Showalter), has obvious relevance of Vandover's decline:

> A man who has been hitherto temperate in all his habits, prudent and industrious in business, and exemplary in the relations of life, undergoes a great change of character, gives way to dissipation of all sorts, launches into reckless speculation in business, and become indifferent to his wife, his family, the obligations of his position; his surprised friends see only the effects of vice and ... after a time, they hear that he is in the police court accused of assault or stealing.... The dissipation, the speculation, and the theft itself were, as they often are, the first symptoms of general paralysis of the insane. (Showalter 1986, pp. 90–91)

As Vandover's disease progresses, his coordination is affected, he discovers that he can no longer draw, and his career as a promising artist is over. The brute that lurks within him, first loosely associated with his libido, then linked to his disease, overpowers his will. As the disease progresses, he has fits in which he paddles around on all fours and barks and howls. Unlike some werewolf novels and films, the emergence of the brute does not endow Vandover with primitive power; it simply marks the degeneration of his nervous system. At the novel's end, Vandover is seen swabbing out filthy rental homes for their landlord—the old Harvard friend who had cheated him—the only occupation possible for him, and it will not last for long since he is destined for an asylum for victims of general paralysis of the insane.

Norris must have known that *Vandover and the Brute* was unpublishable at the turn of the century, though he did send it to a publisher, who promptly rejected it. In 1914, a dozen years after Frank's death at age thirty-one and some twenty years after its composition, his brother Charles, also a novelist, published what is probably a bowdlerized version of the text. Frank's original script of the novel did not survive. By this time, medicine had progressed, syphilis was no longer completely incurable, and it was treated with some success with the dangerous arsenic-derived Savarin. Antibiotics would not arrive until the 1940s, finally offering a cure for syphilis and TB—and which might have saved Frank Norris, who had died of infection from a burst appendix.

Syphilis and TB may take years to dispatch their victims, but what of fast-moving diseases like influenza, yellow fever, or the bubonic plague, which have destroyed major percentages of the population of Europe?[1] Could an even deadlier plague destroy all civilization or leave only scattered remnants of humanity? Mary Shelley asked this question in her long-neglected novel *The Last Man* (1826), now rediscovered in the age of COVID-19, amid a burgeoning industry in plague apocalypse novels and films, many of which use Gothic tropes. In California, the land of health and progress, the disruptive questions were first posed by Jack London in *The Scarlet Plague* (1912). What would it be like to experience the failure of civilization and western migration on the edge of the Pacific? And if there were any survivors, what would life be like for them? George Stewart would develop the premises of London's novella in *Earth Abides* (1949), and a few years after Stewart's fine novel, *I Am Legend* (1954), by Richard Matheson, joins these questions to a re-invention of the vampire tradition and begins a whole new cycle of apocalyptic fiction.

Scarlet Plagues

Jack London's *The Scarlet Plague* and George Steward's *Earth Abides* both describe the destruction of most of humanity by a fast-moving disease that overwhelms our medical resources, leaving only a handful of immune survivors. Both narratives end decades later, with their protagonists as old men, the only ones who can remember our civilization, surrounded by the illiterate, skin-clad savages who are their descendants. Our notions of progress are revealed to be a vain hope, and instead we watch the course of our empire run through its final stages, from *Consummation* to *Destruction* to *Desolation* (in Thomas Cole's sequence). Both protagonists, London's Berkeley literature Professor Smith, and Stewart's Berkeley graduate student Isherwood Williams, meditate upon the cycles of history. While Smith cynically imagines the rediscovery of gunpower eons in the future, empowering again the destructive features of humanity, Isherwood (Ish) laments that the great library of the University of California, still standing, is filled with books that no one will ever read.

London's novella, told from the vantage point of 2073, is the reminiscences of Professor Smith, told to his sometimes incredulous and dismissive grandsons.

In an obvious homage to Poe's "The Masque of the Red Death," Smith describes a group of faculty families barricaded against disease and looters in the university's chemistry building. Of course, the deadly disease breaches their defenses, and the group attempts to escape to the countryside in an ever-shrinking caravan, leaving, finally, only young Smith to reach the isolated splendor of Yosemite. After living for a few seasons on the stored bounty of the park's hotel, he descends to find a handful of survivors in the Bay Area. Now, as he reflects as an old man, everything he valued in his previous life is lost. He lives in a tribe of illiterate hunter-gatherers who collect teeth from the skulls of plague-dead Americans to string as ornaments.

In *Earth Abides*, George Stewart (himself a Berkeley professor) chronicles the years between the calamity of the plague and the protagonist's old age with greater nuance and detail. Isherwood (Ish) returns from a research trip to the Sierra to find Berkeley empty. In the following years, he even tours the country by car and meets a few other survivors before returning home to Berkeley and locating a mate, Emma (Em), and gradually building a family and the nucleus of a tribe of other survivors. For many years, the life of the tribe has been idyllic, as canned food from the largely intact city is plentiful. The literary model here is less Mary Shelley's *The Last Man* than Daniel Defoe's *Robinson Crusoe* (1719). The water supply and electricity eventually fail, but the tribe adapts easily. One of Ish's children, Joey, has a precocious love of learning and brings hope that literacy and even science will survive. The tribe needs little governance and is run by consensus and the gentle leadership of Ish, Em, and two other elders.

The age of lazy innocence ends with the arrival of Charlie, a powerful, charismatic figure that Ish and the leadership instinctively mistrust—a Gothic villain, in fact. Charlie is armed, bullying, and often drunk, and focuses his attention on a beautiful but mentally disabled woman whom the tribe has protected. He also suffers from venereal diseases, as he drunkenly reveals to one of the elders. Envisioning a future in which the tribe's stock is crippled with retardation and congenital syphilis, the elders vote to execute Charlie, which marks the beginning, as Ish realizes, of something like a state. However, Charlie's impact does not end with his hanging and burial. He was also a typhoid carrier, and in the local plague that he introduced, many died, including Ish's precocious son Joey, whom he saw as the tribe's future.

The Scarlet Plague and *Earth Abides* end with similar visions of the postapocalyptic future. The small tribes inhabiting California have no writing and even have forgotten many of the words common in our language. Ish's great-grandson cannot even remember the name of the *coin*, though he knows that the white and brown disks are useful for making arrowheads. Smith was never reconciled to the loss of the pleasures of the old times, such as opera and mayonnaise. Yet the ending of *The Scarlet Plague* undercuts Smith's despair: a Berkeley English professor, an elitist, of course, is an unreliable narrator. *The Scarlet Plague* concludes with an image of horses running on a beach, and then this picture of the sunset:

> The low sun shot red shafts of light, fanshaped, up from a cloud-tumbled horizon. And close at hand in the white waste of shore-lashed waters, the sea-lions, bellowing their old primeval chant, hauled up out of the sea on the black rocks and fought and loved.
> "Come on, Granser," Edwin prompted.
> And old man and boy, skin-clad and barbaric, turned and went along the right of way into the forest in the wake of the goats. (pp. 127–28)

In the beauty of these images—worthy of a poem by Robinson Jeffers—we see something that Professor Smith cannot: the California tribes have achieved a life in harmony with the landscape that our old civilization failed to achieve.

Similarly, as Ish declines into old age, he is aware that his people continue to grow, adapt, and flourish. He is seen as a king, nearly a god, carrying his old geologist's hammer that signifies his authority—though, increasingly senile, his authority is merely symbolic. He dies as he is being carried across the still-standing Bay Bridge as his people migrate from fires in the East Bay to other lands on the Peninsula. Ish's last act is to pass the sacred hammer to a great grandson, a strong young man with wavy blond hair named, of course, Jack. The novel ends with Stewart's tribute to his predecessor.

Names, as others have observed, are important in *Earth Abides* (Willis pp. xiii–xiv). "Ish" is the Hebrew word for man, as Em is for woman. Ish also references Ishmael in both the Bible and in *Moby Dick*: "And I only am escaped alone to tell thee." (Job 1. 15–17; Melville 1983, p. 1408). But it also recalls Ishi, the Yahi Indian who emerged from the Sierra Foothills in 1911. Ishi never told his real name; Ishi means "man" in Yahi, as it does in Hebrew. He has a special significance for Californians, combining guilt and longing, and California writers from Mary Austin to Ursula K. Le Guin have imagined the life Ishi and his tribe once had and lost. London and Stewart suggest that the "savage state" following an apocalypse might represent, finally, a return to a lost home.[1]

Zombies and Vampires

Richard Matheson's *I Am Legend* (1954) was published five years after *Earth Abides* and reflects the anxieties of the Cold War. A war in 1975, barely mentioned, has produced a toxic dust-laden atmosphere that also breeds swarms of disease-bearing insects. The resulting plague has apparently destroyed all human life, except for that of a sole survivor, Robert Neville. Those infected are at first still living creatures longing for human blood; then are the undead, corpses animated by plague bacteria. Thus, as Neville come to understand, vampirism is simply a disease that has coexisted with humanity from the beginning. It was the real disease behind the Black Death and the plague that weakened Athens during the Peloponnesian War. It is not supernatural; stories like *Dracula* embellish with superstition an actual contagion that must be understood empirically.

Neville lives in a nearly intact Los Angeles, and his story, like that of Isherwood, recalls *Robinson Crusoe*. The wrecked ship washed upon the rocks by Crusoe's island, which plentifully supplied him with firearms, gunpowder, tobacco, and rum. So too, Neville mines the stores of the city. Moreover, Crusoe's compound, surrounded by a living palisade with firing ports for his many muskets, anticipates Neville's suburban home, barricaded and stocked with food, a generator, firearms, and whiskey. Crusoe fears an attack by scarcely human cannibals; Neville must defend his fortified home every night from the inhuman creatures who were once his friends and neighbors.

Neville is ultimately defeated by subterfuge as he takes in an apparent fellow survivor, Ruth, who is in fact a member of a vampire group that has learned how to arrest the illness. In the novel's surprise ending, Neville evades his execution by committing suicide. He has himself become the monster in the eyes of this new group of vampires (vampires 2.0), a villain like Charley in *Earth Abides*, and thus will be remembered as the evil that had to be defeated to make way for a new version of humanity.

The ending is unsatisfying to many readers and has been rejected in the two most recent film adaptations. Neville kills the truly dead as well as the still-living infected vampires in ignorance of the emergence of the new vampire condition, but there is no way he could have known. The new group could have communicated with him, but they did not. The soldiers of Vampire 2.0 hunt down the dead, germ-controlled vampires with a brutality that appalls even Neville. "Is this the new society?" he asks (p. 158). Thus, I am not convinced that the new vampire race will be nobler than Neville's extinguished humanity. Nor—with apologies to Agnieszka Soltisik Monnet, who reads the novel differently—am I convinced that Ruth is morally superior to the lewd vampire women who try to lure Neville outside during the nightly siege of his home (Crow *Companion to American Gothic* p. 214).

I Am Legend has had almost no influence on later vampire fiction, which, following Anne Rice and others, has reconnected with the supernatural traditions of Stoker and Le Fanu and has gone in different directions. But Matheson's idea of a disease transforming humans into monsters has had a great impact on fiction and film about zombies. From *The Night of the Living Dead* (1968) to *The Walking Dead* (TV series, 2010-) to *World War Z* (film 2013) to the Korean *Train to Busan* (2016)—slow zombies and fast zombies—we have the trope of besieged humans fighting off hordes of biting, flesh-rending creatures. And all this began in the Los Angeles suburbs.

Disease is a metaphor. In 1954, Los Angeles, what anxieties were expressed in this recurring image of surrounding vampires or zombies? What, then, were we afraid of? Surely then, as now, white suburban dwellers feared mobs of black and brown people who had been excluded and erased from the suburbs. The "Zoot Suit Riots" of the war were still a fresh memory. Mike Davis observes, pointedly, that "the abiding hysteria of Los Angeles disaster fiction, and perhaps all disaster fiction ... is racial anxiety" (p. 281). Bernice Murphy notes that the novel is set in and around Compton, which was in the process of changing from a majority white to a majority African American community (*California Gothic* pp. 79–88), so that the vampires are coded as invading black people. More subtly, this was the era of Joe McCarthy and the House Un-American Activities Committee, who spread the fear of the infiltration of the community by Communist ideas that could "turn" apparently normal citizens into secret zombie-communists, waiting to emerge and overwhelm the American way of life. Jack Finney's science-fiction novel *The Body Snatchers* (1954) and its film adaptations (1956, 1978) draw on this same paranoia.

AIDS Gothic

Finally, a brief excursion into the Marvel Universe. The 1998 film *Blade*, directed by Stephen Norrington and starring Wesley Snipes, is set in Los Angeles—though, admittedly, it could be any metropolis. While *Blade* has been read as an allegory of race in America (Weinstock pp. 213–14), it is also something else. Just as Stoker's *Dracula* was written during a syphilis epidemic, when sexual contact occurred in an atmosphere of fear and suspicion, vampire fiction flourished again in the age of AIDS. Sexuality brought death from incurable disease, as could transfusions with infected blood. *Blade* notably begins with blood spraying from sprinklers in the vampire nightclub, and blood and serums are present in nearly every scene. Blade's love interest, Karen, is a hematologist. At the climax of the film, Deacon Frost's vampires have captured Blade in the Temple of Eternal Night and attempt to drain his blood as a sacrifice to the Blood God, in a rite intended to bring about the vampire apocalypse.

When Karen tells Deacon Frost, "You are a sexually transmitted disease," the key metaphor of the film is revealed. Blade, the Day Walker, is the modified virus as a vaccine that can destroy the disease. The disease is AIDS, the Gothic disease of our time. And, as always, disease is also a metaphor. Here, as in *Angels in America* (1991–92), AIDS is linked to political corruption. In *Blade*, vampires are revealed to control the police, the banks, and the politicians. Fortunately for the producers of the Marvel franchise, it will be a long fight.

The dream of a healthy life in California could never be achieved by everyone. Immigrants brought diseases with them that they could not escape. Beaches and beautiful sunsets could offer no protection from ancient plagues like TB, which may be, in fact, older than humanity (Cartwright 2020, p. 146), influenza, or syphilis. While these and other afflictions may have been beaten back by modern science, new plagues have emerged—HIV, SARS, and COVID-19—from which we are no safer in California than anywhere else. California disease gothic has been an index of hopes and fears, suggesting that we cannot leave human frailty behind, and cannot achieve perfection or immortality. All that may be offered is some hope of renewal beyond a coming apocalypse.

Endnote

1   For the homecoming theme, see my "Homecoming in the California Visionary Romance."

Chapter 5

THE SHADOW LINE: NOIR AND CALIFORNIA GOTHIC

You can never know too much about the shadow line and the people who walk it …

—Raymond Chandler, *The Long Goodbye*

Film noir, like the beautiful but deadly oleander bush, was a European import that took root in California and flourished.

Noir, which was named retroactively by French film critics Raymond Borde and Étienne Chaumeton (Fine in Crow, Companion to American Gothic p. 476), was a style that developed early in the silent era in Germany and Austria. Noir combined an expressionistic aesthetic involving deep shadows and odd-angle shots with a largely Gothic subject matter. Early noir films included such obviously Gothic titles as *The Golem*, *Nosferatu*, and *The Cabinet of Dr. Caligari*. When noir directors, including Paul Wegener, Fritz Lang, Robert Wiene, and F. W. Murnau, fled Nazi Germany in the 1930s, they joined other creative émigrés from Germany and Austria in Southern California. In Hollywood, the expat directors blended their noir aesthetic with plots drawn from hard-boiled crime fiction to create California film noir, which, as David Fine indicates, is "a twentieth-century manifestation of American Gothic, contemporaneous with Southern Gothic fiction" (p. 475).

The scripts for Hollywood film noir were often adaptations of hardboiled crime stories by such alumni of *The Black Mask* as Dashiell Hammett, James M. Cain, Horace McCoy, and Raymond Chandler. Studios, in fact, often employed the authors to adapt their fiction into screenplays. The resulting noir crime films are filled with Gothic tropes: masks and doubles, buried secrets, and the incursion of the past into the present. The ambiance of dread in these screenplays draws in part on the shared traumas of the twentieth century, the Great Depression, and the thirty-year war soon to enter its terrible second act (Scruggs pp. 123–37). But there were also local concerns coloring California noir, including the morbidity of a land of sunshine filled with the sick and the dying, as discussed in Chapter 6, the corruption of local politics and law enforcement that continued despite the reforms of the Progressive Era, and the sex scandals plaguing the film industry. These scandals, as catalogued by Kenneth Anger in his salacious history of *Hollywood Babylon*, were reflected in the erotic charge of many Hollywood movies, even during the era of the Hayes Act.

This chapter will use the term "noir" to describe both noir film and the fiction that exists symbiotically with it. Key film noirs and noir detective fiction from the 1940s to more recent neo-noir will be discussed, with emphasis on Raymond Chandler's *The Lady in the Lake* (1943), Alfred Hitchcock's *Vertigo* (1958), David Lynch's *Mulholland Drive* (2001), Walter Moseley's *The Devil in a Blue Dress* (1990), James Elroy's *The Black Dahlia* (1987), and Thomas Pynchon's *Inherent Vice* (2009). Emphasis will be placed on the women who are variously victims, tempters, and antagonists in these works: their femme fatales. The women drive these plots, and it is their presence that makes them Gothic.

The Imp of the Perverse

At the beginning of Hitchcock's *Vertigo*, Scotty, then a police detective, chases a suspect against the skyline of San Francisco. He slips and falls and grasps a gutter, where he is left dangling as the sequence ends. Critic Robin Wood finds a metaphor for the whole movie in this scene, in its "tension between the desire to fall and the dread of falling … (p. 110). This tension defines Scotty's relationship with Madeline, the film's femme fatale, who "is continually associated with death, and the fascination she exerts is the fascination of death, a drawing toward oblivion and final release …" (p. 114).

Wood does not note that this pattern is embedded in the dark romanticism of American Gothic and was defined by Edgar Allan Poe as "The Imp of the Perverse." Poe's story by that name—which deceives the reader into thinking it is an essay before revealing itself to be the first-person narrative of Poe's usual barking lunatic—asks us to imagine ourselves standing at the edge of a cliff:

> We stand upon the brink of a precipice. We peer into the abyss—we grow sick and dizzy …. And because our reason violently deters us from the brink, *therefore*, do we more impetuously approach it…. Examine these and similar actions as we will, we shall find them resulting solely from the spirit of the *Perverse*. We perpetrate them merely because we feel that we should *not*. (p. 829)

The Imp of the Perverse drives the noir. The noir protagonist stands on a cliff, metaphorically speaking, and takes what he knows is the fatal step, impelled by greed or lust (usually both) or some motive he does not understand. In *Double Indemnity*—both the novel by James M. Cain (1934) and the film adaptation (1946), which offer perfect noir plots—the insurance agent Walter Neff launches off the cliff into a doomed conspiracy to murder Phyllis Dietrichson's husband and collect his insurance. In *Vertigo*, Scotty, against his best judgment and that of the sensible Midge, becomes fatally entangled with the death-haunted Madeline, whose name recalls Poe's Madeline Usher.

The noir detective story weaves together the two stands of Poe's fiction, the Gothic tale and the tale of ratiocination, as Poe called it, that is, the detective story. The detective tries to bring light, clarity, and logic, revealing secrets and uncovering guilt, fitting together the pieces of the puzzle. But his investigations often turn up more and more secrets, sometimes leading into the deep past and sometimes leading to shadows that cannot be dispelled. At the heart of the mystery is the archetypical noir pattern, the fatal choice impelled by the Imp of the Perverse. In Chandler's *The Lady in the Lake*, for example, we glimpse dimly the hidden story—the seduction of Degarmo into a life of crime by the femme fatale we know as Muriel Chess. Degarmo was once a decent cop, according to Bay City (i.e., Santa Monica) Captain Webber, but, as Marlowe reveals, he was lured by Muriel Chess into blackmail and murder, and this ultimately led to the violent deaths of both Chess and Degarmo. Degarmo is the double of Chandler's knight Marlowe—what he might have become had he not left a corrupt system and walked the mean streets alone. Marlowe may stand on the shadow line, but never crosses it to fall into the abyss.

California has often been seen as a place of refuge and renewal. It is a place for starting over, for healing, and for self-fashioning. This belief has motivated generations of women to embark for California, and often for Hollywood, seeking self-fulfillment, glamor, and fame. Of course, they seldom find it. What happens to such women is a major theme of California noir. Instead of a confident heroine, she becomes a victim or a vamp—and the line between them is often hard to draw. Instead of healing and wholeness, the noir woman remains divided or fragmented. Images of mirrors (or broken mirrors) as well as photographs and paintings are frequent in the noir, offering obscure clues as to the femme fatale's identity.

Doubles, Shape Shifters, and the California Uncanny

Thus in Raymond Chandler's *The Lady in the Lake*, Marlowe has a photo of the missing Crystal Kingsley, and the corrupt cop Al Degarmo has a picture of the woman known as Muriel Chess, but they seem indistinguishable. Muriel, the shape-shifting serial murderer, is believed to be the swollen corpse pulled from a lake early in the novel and variously appears as Crystal (whose identity she has assumed), as Mrs. Fallbrook (a brunette who looks nothing like Crystal), and—as the investigation leads into the past—as Mildred Haviland, Dr. Ardmore's nurse and lover, whom Detective Al Degarmo had married. Each new identity corresponds to a murder: of Crystal (the real lady in the lake), of Chris Lavery, and of Florence Ardmore. Ultimately, she may be considered responsible for the death of Degarmo, who died fleeing arrest.

The final confrontation between Muriel (still posing as Crystal) and Marlowe is uncanny. Taking place at night in Muriel's apartment, it is almost a lovers' assignation. When Marlowe reveals that he knows her to be Muriel Chess, their struggle over a gun is like a lover's embrace. Then the hidden Degarmo—Marlow's dark double—knocks Marlowe unconscious and kills Muriel, as if carrying out Marlowe's unacknowledged desire.

Muriel's mystery is never penetrated. The name Chess is appropriate for an antagonist of the chess-playing Marlowe. But we never know her real name, whence she came, or how long her trail of murders might stretch. When Degarmo kills her, he strips her naked and claws at her body with his nails (a strangely unmasculine action), as if trying to peel away her layers of disguise to reach her real identity. Eternally seductive, tempting men to crime, she seems the embodiment of Poe's Imp of the Perverse.

Another shape shifter is Judy Barton, who blends the roles of victim and femme fatale in Alfred Hitchcock's masterpiece, *Vertigo* (1958). She comes to San Francisco with the modest goal of escaping a disagreeable stepfather. She is working in a downtown department store—back in the day when such a humble job would allow you to live in the city—when she is discovered by her evil Pygmalion, Gavin Elster. (It is probably no coincidence that *My Fair Lady*, the musical based on Shaw's play *Pygmalion*, appeared just two years before *Vertigo*.) Elster trains the working-class Judy to dress, talk, and act like his wealthy wife, Madeline, who, in the script he has written for Judy-as-Madeline, is haunted by the tragic story of her great-grandmother, the tragic beauty Carlotta Valdes.

Vertigo is remarkable for the complexity of its Gothic imagery (doubles, towers, corridors, portraits, and mirrors) and for the complexity of its femme fatale. The heroine is a double double: Carlotta, the real Madeline (Ulster's wife), Judy, and Judy-as-Madeline. Judy even has her own Imp-of-the-Perverse moment when she opens the door to Scotty, who has followed her to her shabby hotel room. She knows she should repel him and should step away from the precipice, as she later reveals in her never-sent letter to Scotty. But she lets him in. Judy then becomes a kind of double for Scotty, as each has a complex and impossible love for the other, based on a fantasy of Judy as Madeline.

After Scottie's rediscovery of Judy, he assumes the role of Pygmalion, once played by Elster. He thus becomes a double of the villain, as he makes her yet again into Madeline, even buying her the gray suit that Madeline wore—and that Judy still has buried in her closet. When they climb the mission tower in the final scene, which will result in the second death of Madeline, she speaks nearly incoherently in the instant before her death as both Madeline and Judy, attempting again to convince Scotty of her love.

Robin Woods dismisses the idea, in the scenario created by Elster that Madeline is haunted by Carlotta and stresses that Judy is haunted by Madeline (Wood p. 123). After all, Judy is complicit in the death of Elster's wife, the real Madeline, and bears this guilt. Does she perhaps think that the nun who appears in the tower is Madeline's ghost?

But it is just as viable to insist that Judy, and indeed the whole film, *is* haunted by Carlotta. The story of Carlotta, told by Pop Leibel in the bookshop, is indeed disturbing, and Bernard Herrmann's brilliant musical score evokes Carlotta at intervals, as when we see Carlotta's portrait in the museum, when we notice the spiral pattern of Carlotta's hair echoed in Madeline's, and when we see Carlotta's heirloom necklace around Judy's neck in the mirror—which she wears as she plunges to her death.

Could it then be Carlotta's ghost that Judy sees in the shadows? Or does she see the nun that she, channeling Carlotta, described to Scotty, the cruel Sister Teresa, who chased her away when she played near the mission church as a little girl? We need to consider, in any event, the sketchy history of Carlotta that we learn in the bookshop. The story of Carlotta, born according to her tombstone in 1831, takes us deeper and deeper into California's past: to the days of San Francisco's wild Barbary Coast, to the Mexican and Spanish past of the missions, and at last to California's uncanny, the largely suppressed story of native peoples, that is the ultimate source of the Gothic in *Vertigo*: for Carlotta, the beautiful, sad, and mad Carlotta from the mission, herself remade by an earlier evil Pygmalion, must have carried Indian blood.

The Dahlia

Vertigo and *The Lady in the Lake* both appeared in the mid-century, the 30s, 40s, and 50s being the classic period of first-generation California noir. This was a period of social disruption and population influx for the state, especially during the war years. Among the seekers then was a girl named Elizabeth (or Betty) Short, from Medford, Massachusetts, who had hoped, of course, to find fame in Hollywood. She took screen tests but drifted into LA's demimonde and often claimed to be the wife, fiancée, or widow of a serviceman. She made few friends but was remembered by other young women with whom she shared rooms for her distinctive appearance. She dyed her brown hair a dead black and always wore black clothing—a Goth costume, as we would now see it. Her casual acquaintances gave her a nickname that echoed a popular noir film, *The Blue Dahlia* (1946). They called her the Black Dahlia.

Elizabeth Short was found on a vacant lot in Los Angeles on January 15, 1947. Her nude body had been cut in two and bore evidence of mutilation and torture before her death. Her pale body had been drained of blood, as if, some noted, by a vampire. In bitter irony, she had indeed found fame at the age of twenty-two, in what would be the most notorious unsolved murder case in the history of Los Angeles. As Kevin Starr summarizes:

> Desperate, terrible, obscene in its cruelty, the Black Dahlia case mesmerized Los Angeles throughout January and February of 1947 not only because of its graphic horrors but because ... the brief and unhappy life of Elizabeth Short said something about Los Angeles itself: something about the anonymity, the desperation, the cruelty and brutality life could have in the City of Angels. (Starr 2002, *Embattled*, p. 221)

The Black Dahlia cast a long shadow over California and would remain the most infamous Filmland crime until the murder of Sharon Tate and four others by the Manson family cult in 1969. Whenever a starry-eyed innocent is portrayed arriving in the Southland, hungry for glamor and success, the ghost of the Dahlia is never far away. She is present, though never directly referenced, in David Lynch's *Mulholland Drive*, when Betty (*short* for Elizabeth) arrives at the train station in Los Angeles, telling the kindly older couple about her screen test. We know this will not end well, though we have no idea of the twists and turns and Gothic doublings that are in store for us.

Among the literary adaptations of Betty Short's story, the most intense is surely James Elroy's The *Black Dahlia* (1987). Elroy tells us in the afterword to the novel, as well as in his memoir *My Dark Places* (1996), that the story of Elizabeth Short was interwoven in his imagination with the rape and murder of his own mother, Geneva (or Jean) Hilliker—another small-town girl who came to Los Angeles.[1]

Jean Hilliker was killed in 1958, when Elroy was ten years old. On his eleventh birthday, he met the Black Dahlia: "She came to me in a book. An innocent gift burned my world down." (*Places* p. 101) The book was a gift from his father: *The Badge* (1958) by Jack Webb, the creator and star of the popular radio and TV police procedural *Dragnet*. Webb's collection of true crimes "that could not be presented on TV," as it said on the cover, included, of course, the murder of Elizabeth Short. Elroy read, "read the Dahlia story a hundred times ... Betty Short became my obsession. And my symbolic stand-in for Geneva Hilliker Elroy" (p. 103).

Young Elroy drifted into delinquency, alcoholism, drug use, and petty crime. He did some jail time. Eventually, he reformed his life, began to write, and created the book for which his life and obsessions had been preparing him: "I wrote my novel and sold it. It was all about L.A. crime and me" (p. 154). Later, as he tells us in *My Dark Places*, he secured the help of a senior Los Angeles County Sheriff's Department detective and reopened the case of Jean Hilliker. Despite some new evidence, the mysterious "swarthy man," last seen with his mother and presumably her killer, was never found.

Considering Elroy's paired obsessions, it is inevitable that doubling, body horror, and sexual taboos are Gothic tropes found everywhere in *The Black Dahlia*. The murder is investigated by two detectives who are former boxers, Lee and Bucky (Mr. Fire and Mr. Ice). The girl obsessively loved by Bucky and Lee in a strange *ménage à trois*, Kate, also shares with Elizabeth a life in Los Angeles's sleazy demimonde, from which Lee had rescued her. The novel's femme fatale, Madeline—whose name recalls characters by both Poe and Hitchcock—not only resembles the Dahlia, but is obsessed with her, had met her, and sometimes dresses in Dahlia Goth style to cruise the bars frequented by the dead Elizabeth. The Dahlia, in death, exerts a fascination like Poe's Imp of the Perverse, drawing women into her dark Gothic underworld.

The body horror of the narrative encompasses not only the graphic description of the mutilated Dahlia but Bucky's excavation of Lee's corpse in Mexico and the grotesque fight among jars of human body parts in formaldehyde at the site of Elizabeth's torture and death. Taboos are broken everywhere in the narrative, including Madeline's carnal relationship with her father, which is only partially mitigated by the revelation that he is not her biological father.

Elroy exposes more of the corruption of the police than even Chandler and details the relationship between the department and organized crime—a subject he would take up again in *L.A. Confidential* (1990). Elroy's LAPD is another world altogether from Jack Webb's propagandistic *Dragnet*. Bucky, working alone, solves the case of the Black Dahlia and that of his partner Lee's murder. But he is forced out of the police and leaves for a new life with Kate in the East.

Elroy's solution, like that of John Gregory Dunne's Dahlia novel, *True Confessions* (1977), is (barely) plausible; it involves fictional characters layered onto a foundation of fact. Madeline, her parents, and her father's abused and crazed friend never existed. We read the novel with the knowledge that the Dahlia's real killer, like Jean Hilliker's Swarthy Man, was never found.

Black LA Noir

The femme fatale of Walter Moseley's *Devil in a Blue Dress* (1990), Daphne Monnet, is another shape shifter with multiple identities. She brings into the world of L.A. noir the Southern Gothic themes of concealed genealogy and racial passing.

Devil in a Blue Dress is the origin story of Ezekiel (Easy) Rawlings, the hero of a subsequent series of noir detective novels. Coming to Los Angeles from Houston to work in the aircraft industry, Rawlings hopes to refashion himself as a skilled worker and homeowner and to escape the life of crime he was being drawn into in Houston by his gangster friend Mouse. Houston represents the past, and it will not be repressed. Mouse is a kind of double for Easy, representing black rage—a familiar figure in black American literature and life. When Rawlings loses his job at an aircraft company and accepts the apparently simple task of finding the missing Daphne, Mouse reappears, a force of violence and chaos that Easy both needs and deplores.

All the black characters in the novel come to Los Angeles (or specifically to Watts) from Houston, the city of the past. So too does Daphne: adversary, victim, murderess, tempter, and Moseley's Imp of the Perverse.

The novel is set in 1948, the year after the Black Dahlia murder. Though the case is not explicitly mentioned, there is a sly allusion when Rawlins, asking about Daphne but pretending to forget her name, calls her "Dahlia."

Like her name (which is not really Daphne), everything about the woman is ambiguous. Later, Rawlins will say that "Daphne was like the chameleon lizard. She changed for her man" (*Devil* 186). When Rawlins first begins his search for Daphne, he has only a photograph—a realistically plausible detail but also a Gothic trope. The photograph, Rawlins recognizes, appears to be an original black-and-white image that has been artificially colored. This is the first hint of Daphne's suppressed genealogy. When Mouse calls her "Ruby," the truth emerges, for Mouse knew her as a child in Houston, the site of the novel's buried secrets. Daphne/Ruby tells Rawlins that she became the lover of her father after visiting a zoo and watching zebras mate:

> I'm not Daphne. My given name is Ruby Hanks and I was born in Lake Charles, Louisiana. I'm different than you because I'm two people. I'm her *and* I'm me. I never went to that zoo, she did. She was there and

that's where she lost her father. I had a different father. He came home and fell in my bed about as many times as he fell in my mother's. He did that until one night Frank killed him. (*Devil* p. 207)

Frank is Daphne's black half-brother, not her boyfriend, as people in Watts have assumed.

Rawlins does not entirely believe this story, and the symbolism of copulating zebras seems too obvious a symbol. Nonetheless, the history of childhood sexual abuse, if it is true, explains her role as an avenging angel when she murders the corrupt politician and pedophile Teran.

Rawlins is drawn to this Imp of the Perverse, though he considers her "the devil" (p. 148). He thinks that "Daphne Monet was death herself" (p. 208). But he enjoys a long night of raw sex with her—a scene that does not make it into the film version with Denzel Washington and Jennifer Beals. In the end, Daphne disappears, with help from Rawlins, and she leaves him money that she had extorted from Teran: money that Rawlins uses to pay off his mortgage, buy some property, and begin his career as a private eye. The ambiguous femme fatale is as essential as the murderous mouse in creating the complex hero that Rawlins becomes.

The film *The Devil in the Blue Dress* is a neo-noir, shot in color but developing the themes of the classic black-and-white movies that defined the genre. Hitchcock's *Vertigo* had shown the way. Neo-noir films still favored the early and mid-century settings of the earlier noir, however. Polanski's Chinatown (1974), one of the finest neo-noir films, was set in the 1930s and employs to brilliant effect political corruption and a buried family secret. Even Robert Altman's 1973 riff on Chandler's *The Long Goodbye* (1953), though nominally moved to the 1970s, depicts Marlowe (played by Elliot Gould) driving a classic first-generation Lincoln Continental from the 1940s—nearly a match for Faye Dunaway's gorgeous Packard convertible in *Chinatown*.

Moving toward the century's end and beyond, noir cinema continued to quote from the classics of earlier decades and even reference the Black Dahlia; however, different cultural traumas, especially from the end of the turbulent 1960s (the Matter of the Sixties), provided new touchstones.

Silencio

David Lynch's *Mulholland Drive* (2001) is a complex, multi-layered film about the Gothic underside of the movie business. Its very title and opening recall Billy Wilder's Gothic classic *Sunset Boulevard* (1950). When Rita flees the car crash that killed her would-be assassins, she stumbles down the hillside until she reaches Sunset, where she enters the house where she will meet Betty:

a clear homage to the beginning of Wilder's film, where Joe Gillis, evading the repo men who are trying to seize his car, turns into the driveway of Norma Desmond's mansion. Gillis finds a haunted house in which the still-living specters of Hollywood's silent film era gather. *Mulholland Drive* offers its own glimpses into the world of Hollywood directors and stars and the incursions of organized crime, but it is more concerned with the other end of the Hollywood spectrum, the sad lives of the young women who try to break into the glamorous life of movie stars. The ghost of the Dahlia always hovers over such stories.

When we first meet Betty, she seems, indeed, on the verge of realizing the Hollywood dream. She has won a screen test as the prize in a jitterbug contest in her Canadian hometown, and an aunt, already connected with Hollywood, has lent her a lovely apartment. The appearance of the amnesiac Rita brings not only romance but also a girl-detective adventure that may unlock the mystery of Rita's past. At her screen test, Betty turns the clichéd lines she and Rita had laughed at into a smoldering, sexually charged encounter that will launch Betty's career—as on another level, it launched that of the actress portraying Betty, the then obscure Naomi Watts. As Betty leaves the audition, a chance encounter with the director, Adam Kesher, hints at the direction her life might take.

Such miraculous fortune is too good to be true, obviously. About two-thirds of the way through the film, after Betty and Rita visit the Club Silencio, we are forced to re-evaluate everything we have seen and realize that most of it has been the fantasy of an aspiring actress named Diane Selwyn, who lives in a dismal apartment, has broken up with her rather unattractive girlfriend, and will take her own life, resulting in another sad story of broken dreams.

Mulholland Drive gestures toward many earlier films, and especially *Vertigo*, "the most famous twice-told tale in American cinema" (Lim 2015, p. 156). In each, the audience witnesses the conflict between glamor and reality in the soul of the heroine, leading to the destruction of both women.

Inherent Vice and the End of the Sixties

Thomas Pynchon's detective hero, Larry "Doc" Sportello, drifts through *Inherent Vice* in a haze of marijuana snoke. But, though a hippy and a stoner, he is, in fact, a competent detective, a crack shot, a relentless investigator, and (like Chandler's Marlowe) above all, loyal to his clients. He is also a trickster, in the tradition of Odysseus, Br'er Rabbit, and Bugs Bunny, whose tagline ("What's up, Doc?) Sportello's nickname evokes. When he is handcuffed and about to be injected with a fatal overdose of heroin, he escapes from his cuffs, beats and chokes one of his kidnappers to death, and fatally wounds the other.

Inherent Vice is, in its bones, a self-consciously traditional noir detective story with references to Chandler, Hammett, *The Postman Always Rings Twice*, *Vertigo*, and the Black Dahlia. It begins, like so many noir stories, with a girl asking for the favor of a detective. The girl, Shasta Faye, is Doc's former lover, the novel's femme fatale, and a symbol of a passing era. The favor she asks draws him into an endless series of complications, which—this being a Pynchon novel—lead to a paranoid realm of conspiracies involving a cabal of mysterious but eternally present powerful men, here represented by Crocker Fenway. "We've been in place forever," Fenway explains to Doc, "Look around. Real estate, water rights, oil, cheap labor—all of that's ours, it's always been ours. And you, at the end of the day what are you" (*Vice* p. 34)? At the heart of Doc's investigations lies a mystery that cannot be understood. We know that the Golden Fang is a ship, a drug cartel, an office building, an organization with links to the government and to Crocker's cabal— but beyond that we are grasping at shadows.

Nonetheless, Doc succeeds in most of the tasks to which Shasta's request for a favor has led him. Micky Wolfman is freed from the asylum. The hapless trombone player Coy Harlingen is freed from his entanglement as a police informer and returns to his family. There is even a resolution, of a sort, in Doc's difficult relationship with "Bigfoot" Bjornsen, the square, crewcut police detective who is Doc's alter ego. The two men Doc killed were the murderers of Bjornsen's partner, and the policeman, following his own code of justice and revenge, had spun the plot that led to that encounter. Doc's relationship with Bigfoot is as complex as any in the novel, except that with Shasta Faye.

What Doc cannot do is win back Shasta or turn back the clock to the time when they lived together in stoner happiness at Gordita Beach. In this, the novel differs from the excellent film adaptation of *Inherent Vice*, directed by Paul Thomas Anderson (2014), in which Doc and Shasta are reunited. But Pynchon's Shasta is last seen walking away from Doc on the beach: "Doc followed the prints of her bare feet already collapsing into rain and shadow, as if in a fool's attempt to find his way back into a past that despite them both had gone on into the future." (p. 314). Shasta's footprints on the sands of time are those of an era irrevocably lost, as lost as the fabled island of Lemuria or the Indians whose spirits haunt Gordita Beach.

Pynchon sets *Inherent Vice* in 1970. The trial of Charles Manson and his followers, which the author references repeatedly, was about to begin.

The murder of pregnant actress Sharon Tate and four others in August 1969 eclipsed the Black Dahlia as the most infamous of Hollywood crimes. The imagination of the public, inflamed not only by the crime itself but also by the testimony at the trial, was captivated by the idea of a hippy cult leader somehow transforming normal middle-class girls into mass murderers.

The cult guru became the new face of fear in America, and any man with a beard or any barefoot girl was suspect.

And so the hippy era ended. The 1960s, as we remember them, were invented in California, and one version of the California dream ended at Cielo Drive in Beverly Hills, just a short trip up Benedict Canyon from Sunset Boulevard.

Endnote

1 Michael Connolly gives this background—a mother raped and murdered—to his detective hero, Harry Bosch.

Chapter 6

CALIFORNIA ECOGOTHIC: WHAT'S BURIED IN THE BASEMENT

All of history is a rehearsal for its own extinction.

—Cormac McCarthy, *The Passenger*

Ecogothic is based on the knowledge that human activity has changed the planet's climate and biosphere and that the extinction of human and much animal life is likely, if not inevitable. Ecogothic thus looks backward and forward: forward to an apocalypse, backward to what we have done—and the knowledge that we have repressed or ignored.[1]

The ecological disaster, the accelerating Sixth Extinction, is a global concern and not particular to California's magic island. But novels and films about global collapse slot easily into the rich tradition of the California apocalypse, and especially the destruction of Los Angeles, or what Mike Davis has called (in the title of his 1998 book) the "ecology of fear." Los Angeles has been destroyed more than any other city, even more than Tokyo, by earthquake, alien invasion, zombies, plague, and every other imaginable means. But increasingly, the agency of destruction does not have to be imagined but merely observed. As we contemplate the end of our familiar world, we also re-evaluate our received notions of natural history, as embodied in institutions like museums and zoos, and we reconsider California's long tradition of nature writing and celebration of its unique landscape.

This chapter will examine two novels of the near future that imagine the disaster that awaits: Octavia Butler's *Parable of the Sower* (1993) and Claire Vaye Watkins' *Gold Fame Citrus* (2015). In contrast, Lydia Millet's Ecogothic trilogy, *How the Dead Dream* (2008), *Ghost Lights* (2011), and *Magnificence* (2012), is set in the present and is a meditation on how humanity's destructive relationship with the animal world has brought us to this point.

The prescient Octavia Butler (1947–2006) understood before most novelists that climate change would crash infrastructure and civil order and send populations fleeing as refugees. Los Angeles, always fragile, perched on an edge between a desert interior and undrinkable salt water, dependent on stretched arteries bringing water from distant sources, would be an early victim of a hotter and dryer world. The teen-age protagonist of *Parable of the Sower*, Lauren Olamina, remembers a rain shower in which the delighted child played—a wonder seldom repeated. Now, in a time of endless drought and social collapse, ordinary people live in barricaded communities and venture out into the chaos in armed groups. Some of Lauren's neighbors relinquish their freedom and join a work colony, a voluntary slavery run by a Japanese, German, and Canadian corporation. Bands of drug-crazed skinheads called Pyros, driven to orgiastic pleasure by flame, set fires every night, creating a slow-motion version of "The Burning of Los Angeles," the nightmare that has haunted the city since it was visualized in Nathanael West's *The Day of the Locust* (1939). The President of the United States is named Donner, an obvious portent.

Butler's fiction often patrols the borderland between the human and the alien, from her Xenogenesis trilogy to the vampire tale *Fledgling* (2005), her last novel. Her heroines have sex with alien species, and this, with a frequent and creepy hint of pedophilia, is a challenging and thoroughly Gothic strain in her fiction. In *Parable of the Sower*, Lauren is not exactly a mutant, but she suffered a genetic change from drugs ingested by her mother during pregnancy. Consequently, she is deeply empathetic and literally experiences any pain she witnesses. This is not an effective survival trait in an apocalyptic landscape filled with suffering, where she ultimately must fight off and kill vicious attackers, but it makes her not less but more human, or at least more humane, than "normal" people.

Writing in the era after the Manson killings, Butler takes a daring turn by making her heroine the founder of a religious cult. In defiance of her father, a Protestant minister, Lauren develops a belief system called "Earthseed," based on force and change (with a debt to Schopenhauer, perhaps) and a recognition that human life must leave this broken planet. "The Destiny of Earthseed," Lauren teaches, "Is to take root among the stars" (p. 78).

When Lauren's compound is stormed by murderous Pyros and her family is killed, Lauren sets out on foot with two other survivors for Northern California, where, they hope, a new life may be found. She gathers other wanderers, a racially diverse group, including a man who, at fifty-seven, is old enough to be the teenaged Lauren's grandfather and whom she takes as a lover. (Again, the hint of pedophilia.) She teaches her Earthseed religion to her followers, who come to number, inevitably, twelve. The little band defends itself against a Pyro attack and flees a fire the Pyros have set through the Northern California hills near Clear Lake before finding relative safety in an isolated area south of the Lost Coast.

As Jason Haslam has noted, Butler is haunted by the memory of slavery (about which she writes in *Kindred* [1979]), and this haunting infuses *Parable of the Sower* (pp. 54–57). When the American Dream and the California Dream collapse, echoes of the bad old times are everywhere. Lauren's odyssey northward recalls Harriet Tubman leading bands of escaped enslaved people to the promised land across the Ohio River. The bearded Bankole, Lauren's mature lover, is compared to Frederick Douglass.

Parable of the Sower ends with Lauren founding an Earthseed colony. The reader will need its sequel, *Parable of the Talents* (1998), to learn what happened to Lauren's disciples and how she worked to bring out humanity's escape from its doomed planet. Butler did not live to write a planned third volume.

Claire Vaye Watkin's *Gold Fame Citrus* describes another odyssey from a ruined Los Angeles. Its heroine, Luz Dunn, is a one-time B-list model, hapless and indecisive, recalling perhaps Maria Wyeth, the heroine in *Play It as It Lays* (1970) by Joan Didion, whose cold-eyed, ironic sensibility is often felt here. Yet Watkin's novel—her first—is a highly original, kaleidoscopic work, blending Gothic and magic realism, and other elements in this imagining of the end of California and American westering.

In a desiccated landscape from which most inhabitants have long since fled or been forcibly evacuated, Luz Cortez lives with her boyfriend Ray in the ruined home of a former "starlet," wearing the starlet's clothes, jewelry, and designer scarves. She has become, she realizes, "basically another woman's ghost" (p. 6). As such, living in the detritus of Hollywood glamor, she is the heir to all the ruined hopes of generations of young women who sought fame in Hollywood, whom we have seen in Elizabeth Short (the Black Dahlia) and Lynch's Betty Elms.

Watkins invests Luz Dunn with a nearly allegorical significance, associating her with people and events from California's heroic past and the dismal future the author predicts for it. Her name as a model, Luz Cortez, links her with the European discovery of California in the 1540s. She carries about with her a little library that includes biographies of Sacagawea, who guided the Lewis and Clark expedition; of John Westley Powell, who explored the Colorado River (pronounced dead in Luz's lifetime); and the writings of John Muir. Muir, especially, is another ghost that haunts the narrative. His beloved Yosemite is now just a "dry, ruined chasm ringed by hot granite knobs" (p. 77).

As a baby, Luz was selected by the Bureau of Conservation as a mascot and became "Conservation's golden child (10)," the poster baby for another vast and doomed water project. Her name became a catchphrase in the increasingly ironic headlines in Luz's scrapbook: "GOVENOR SIGNS HSB 4579; EVERT SWIMMING POOL IN CALIFORNIA TO BE DRAINED BEFORE BABY DUNN IS OLD ENOUGH TO TAKE SWIMMING

LESSONS ... BERKELEY HYROLOGISTS: WITHHOUT EVACS BABY DUNN WILL DIE OF THIRST BY 24" (pp. 10–11). Luz thus became "the goddesshead of a land whose rape was in full swing before she was even born" (p. 12).

Luz and Ray, the gaunt and bearded boyfriend who resembles John Muir, decide to escape California in the starlet's vintage Karmann Gia, taking with them the toddler they have rescued, or kidnapped, from an abusive group of druggies, seeking moister climes in the Midwest or East. The ironies are obvious, evoking the Oakies fleeing the dust bowl for a new life in the 1930s. Now Californians, fleeing the failed golden state, are known as "Mojavs" and are despised refugees east of the hundredth meridian.

To reach safe and moist lands, Ray, Luz, and the baby Ig must skirt the Armargosa Dune Sea, a vast desert of sand that has spread from the Central Valley and the Mojave Desert, growing ever broader and higher, overtopping even existing mountain ranges. The Dune Sea seems literally improbable, a piece of magic realism, but it is a powerful symbol at the center of the narrative, composed of sand scoured from the once-irrigated farmlands of the Sacramento and San Joaquin Valleys. When their car runs out of fuel, Ray hikes off to find help, and Luz and the toddler Ig, near death, are rescued by members of a cult living on the fringes of the Dune Sea.

The cult is led by the charismatic Levi Zabriskie, who pretends to be a dowser, able to find water in the sterile dunes. In reality, he and his henchmen loot water from government relief convoys. His name evokes Zabriskie Point in Death Valley, and, obviously, Zabriskie is intended to evoke Charles Manson. He, like Manson, controls his "family" with a mixture of personal charm, conspiracy theories, sex, and narcotics. We read about this family with the uneasy knowledge that Claire Vaye Watkin's father, Charles Watkins, was a member of the Manson family—though he was never indicted in the Tate-La Bianca massacre.

When Ray returns, Luz and Ray are nearly burned to death in a fire set by Levi (which burns Luz's westering library), and Ray is beaten by the family. However, they are freed by Levi and sent on their way in a truck given to them by the family. When a freak thunderstorm creates a flash flood, Luz steps out of the floating truck into the torrent.

During her last moments, Luz recalls all the Californians who are her people: "Antsy pioneers, con artists and sooners, dowsers and gurus, Pentecosts and Scientologists, Muscle heads, pill-poppers, pep talkers, drama queens and commuters" (*Citrus* pp. 336–37) and so on for two pages, all the Californians. She has become the last version of Queen Califia, a representative of a civilization that has failed because it destroyed California and the west and sucked it dry until it died. Fittingly, Luz dies when nature takes its revenge.

In a flashback to Levi Zabriskie's earlier days, before he becomes a cult leader, he is shown in Albuquerque, where he encounters a stopped train that contains the animals of a zoo that are being shipped to the east. "Levi felt immense grief at the zoo creatures leaving" and feels that they are in some way "calling to him" (*Citrus* p. 152). This call leads him ultimately to a set of mad beliefs and to his imaginary bestiary of fabulous creatures that inhabit the Dune Sea, as he reveals to Luz. But there was validity in his epiphany by the train tracks. He senses, deeply and emotionally, the great loss of animal life on the planet due to human crimes. This insight is at the core of Lydia Millet's trilogy, *How the Dead Dream* (2009), *Ghost Lights* (2011), and *Magnificence* (2013). Like Watkins, Millet looks back at humanity's crimes against the lives of our fellow creatures and the ways we have tried to justify them.

Down the Rabbit Hole

I propose to examine Millet's trilogy as a re-envisioning of the American tradition of frontier Gothic, though these novels are set in the recent past, the 1990s, and sited mostly in California and Belize.

The term "Frontier Gothic" was given prominence by the 1993 critical collection by that name, edited by David Mogen, Scott P. Sanders, and Joanne B. Karpinski. Both terms in the title, as well as other related terms such as "border," "western," and even "American," have been questioned and complicated by scholars subsequently: one thinks of studies by Krista Comer and Neil Campbell, of María Del Pilar Blanco's *Ghost-Watching American Modernity*, and of studies by International Gothic Society members, such as the collection *Eco-Gothic* edited by William Hughes and Andrew Smith. Nonetheless, the essential perception of Mogen's *Frontier Gothic* remains valid. At the "heart of the indigenous frontier story [Mogen writes in his introduction] was the encounter with the wilderness, an encounter which historically was violent, consuming, intrinsically metaphysical, and charged with paradox and emotional ambivalence" (p. 15).

But what does "nature" mean when there is little, if any, true wilderness left in the world? We are living in what Elizabeth Kolbert calls "The Sixth Extinction" and have come to understand that the elimination of animal species and habitat, accelerating toward some tragic conclusion in our own time, began with our earliest human ancestors. As Lydia Millet says, we package and institutionalize the "remnants of wildness, remnants of what had once been the world" in institutions such as natural history museums and zoos—which are, in essence, miniaturized frontiers (*Magnificence* 224). These institutions, frequently referenced and described by Millet, were first created in their modern forms to celebrate the triumphant march of progress. Now many observers, including Millet, see their dark or Gothic side. They are deeply compromised in their willed innocence and even complicit in the extinction of animal species.

Millet will evoke many tropes of the frontier and the Gothic, beginning with the titles *How the Dead Dream* and *Ghost Lights*. The last novel, *Magnificence*, is set in a haunted house concealing a secret legacy in its basement. Yet her key trope is to define the line between living creatures and extinction as a Gothic frontier.

The trilogy begins with a western migration. The protagonist, Thomas Stern, known always as "T," is a young financial genius, already a self-made millionaire in his early twenties, who decides to move to California in search of further wealth in real estate. As he drives his Mercedes from Palm Springs into the inland empire, he imagines the ghosts of past western tycoons:

> He could almost detect their quaint presence in gas stations along the barest stretches of the freeway. There behind the counter, where sparkles in the white formica leant an air of yesteryear, sat a disheveled Howard Hughes bent over a bottle of milk; or there behind the newspaper rack stood William Randolph Hearst, paging through a tabloid. He grew to see greatness in open space, which fosters the illusion of a last frontier .... (*Dream* pp. 28–29)

T has always believed that "it was only money that could set a person free" (p. 14) and that "honesty was useful chiefly within the confines of the self" (*Dream* p. 15). With great intelligence and strength of will, devoid of hypocrisy or inhibitions, he is a force recalling the naturalistic superman Frank Cowperwood in Theodore Dreiser's "Trilogy of Desire." But T's self-conception and purity of purpose begin to crumple in the Chapter 2, which begins "He killed her driving to Las Vegas" (p. 35).

This death is not that of a woman, but of a coyote struck by T's Mercedes. When the animal dies in T's arms, it is a transforming moment, introducing T to the world of animals, relationships, emotion, and loss. Other disturbing moments follow: he adopts a dog, which is later kidnapped and tortured by a business rival; he finds a perfect lover, Beth, who dies of a heart attack; his mother slides into early dementia, and eventually she will be unable to recognize her son. Then T is told that the retirement community he is building in the desert may destroy the last colony of a species of inoffensive little mammal called the kangaroo rat.

Earlier in the novel, T watches his mother work a jigsaw puzzle that depicts, in evolutionary terms, the ages of man from *Australopithecus* to

Homo sapiens—an image probably taken from a museum diorama. He recalls his childhood faith in progress but now understands that "To love posterity and the great institutions, you had to believe in the wisdom of men. You had to love them as a child might, gazing upward" (p. 117). Now he believes that "all men are childish," but "They still had their institutions, and those institutions still had their beauty ... He loved them nonetheless, even as they declined" (p. 138). Later, as he tries to understand the loss of habitat and species to which he has contributed, he turns to one of these great institutions, the zoo.

Thus begins a mad phase of T's life when his daytime activities in finance are a cover for his obsession with breaking into zoos around the country and sleeping among the animals. In a zoo, he is "drawn to the wildness it contained—how far this was from the realm of his competence. He wanted to meet it." Above all, he must know those animals on the verge of extinction, which are (in a key simile) "at the forefront of aloneness, like pioneers" (p. 135).

However, T's attempt to find rational or mystical insight in zoos fails. He concludes that "The zoos were a holding pen: they had the appearance of gardens, the best of them, but they were mausoleums" (p. 197). "Where the large and wide-ranging animal were concerned, more often than not there was little to find there besides illness. Long ago, they had lost everything and gone mad" (p. 198). He comes to feel, with horror, the "deep rage" (p. 199) of the elephants and leaves zoos forever.

T's disillusionment mirrors that of zoo reformer David Hancocks, whose book *A Different Nature* (2001) is referenced by Millet in her acknowledgements. Zoos, Hancocks writes, "are stark portrayals of our confused relationship with the other animals with which we share the planet" (p. xvii). The usual defenses for the existence of zoos, that is, recreation, research, and conservation, are fraudulent. Only education is a valid excuse for zoos, and this only happens when animals are shown in a recreated natural setting, and this only as a means of encouraging action to preserve or restore their actual original habitat. In this way, zoo animals can at least serve as ambassadors from their world to ours.

So, it is not surprising that the last section of *How the Dead Dream* is set in the wilderness—though the wilderness is a jaguar preserve in Belize that exists by government authority and can be reached easily by road in a few hours from the coast. However, T's upriver journey by boat with a guide is a true Frontier Gothic experience, which is, in David Mogen's words, "an encounter" with the wilderness that is "violent, consuming, intrinsically metaphysical, and charged with paradox and emotional ambivalence" (p. 15). This nightmare in the bush recalls works by Joseph Conrad, Graham Greene, and Robert Stone, and perhaps also contains a distant echo of Theodore Roosevelt's disastrous 1913–14 expedition to find the headwaters of the

Rio da Duvida (the River of Doubt) in Brazil and follow it to the Amazon. T is channeling TR.

When his guide dies and his boat is disabled, T must try to walk out of the jungle. At the novel's end, T is exhausted, starved, dehydrated, and feverish. As he loses consciousness, he believes that a small animal is snuggling against him, perhaps a lost young wild pig, seeking its mother. The image recalls T earlier with the dying coyote and with his injured dog. As we close *How the Dead Dream*, we do not know if T will survive his frontier experience. We do not learn of T's fate, in fact, until the middle of *Ghost Lights*, when Hal, the husband of T's secretary, finds T living, Crusoe-like, on an island, now thin, bearded, and looking like "a mountain man or a hippy" (Millet 2011, *Ghost Lights*, p. 145).

In *Ghost Lights*, Millet's interests shift to larger American institutions, although the natural world of Belize—the rain forests and the ecological tourist areas of the coast—is always present. Hal, the novel's protagonist, is an Internal Revenue Service Investigator and has his own childlike faith in "great institutions" and "the wisdom of men." When he arrives on the coast of Belize, he has little notion of how to search for the missing T. During his investigations, he learns of an illegal airstrike by American forces against rebel Mayan tribesmen who have crossed the border from Guatemala.

Hal, the innocent American who believes in the benevolence of his government, reports this violation of international law to the embassy in Belize City. Shortly afterwards, he is stabbed in what will be reported as mugging and, in a sad echo of the ending of *How the Dead Dream*, bleeds out in a gutter while a stray dog laps his blood. We are left to draw our own conclusions about the benevolence of American institutions.

In the final volume, the protagonist is Hal's widow and T's secretary, Susan. *Magnificence* is a haunted house story that extends Millet's exploration of the living and the extinct and of the institutions we have built on that borderland.

Susan inherits a mansion from a dimly remembered great-uncle. The house and its extensive grounds are in Pasadena, which has been, since the days of Raymond Chandler, a favored site of Southern California Gothic.[2] Her first impression of the interior of the house is that it is "a magician's stage, a goth bordello" (p. 57). A later visitor says, "It's totally Natural History Museum … Circa 1950" (p. 123). The house, through its several floors and many rooms and galleries, is filled with stuffed animals from around the world, often arranged in painted dioramas.

As Susan walks the halls of the mansion, trying to understand her great-uncle's obsession, we are implicitly asked to consider the meanings of natural history museums like the American Museum of Natural History in New York, which the mansion mimics. This museum and others like it were built as temples to our secular religion of progress. They celebrated the triumphant emergence of modern humanity and our dominion over the world. As Donna Haraway notes, on visiting the museum, "One is entering a space that sacralizes democracy, Protestant Christianity, adventure, science, and commerce" (p. 27). Viewing the American Museum of Natural History, one finds the walls inscribed with the words of Theodore Roosevelt: "There are no words that can tell the hidden spirit of the wilderness, that can reveal its mystery.... The nation behaves well if it treats its natural resources as assets which it must turn over to the next generation increased and not impaired in value" (Haraway 1989, pp. 27–28). Inside, the visitor (who, as Donna Haraway notes, seems imagined as a wonder-struck white boy) will encounter animals mounted by Carl Akeley, the father of modern taxidermy, and arranged in elaborate and beautiful dioramas. The dioramas are in the style of realism but are in fact idealized, with the best specimens perfectly restored and arranged, typically in family groups, with a dominant male, females, and young pictured in their peaceful locale. We white boys wander through a reconstructed Eden, absorbing lessons about our stewardship of natural resources and, more subtly, the heroism of mighty hunters like Theodore Roosevelt and Carl Akeley, for whom big game hunting was apparently a rite of passage into manly citizenship and who made the museum possible.

Now we may find a museum to be, in the words of David Hancocks, "dark halls of shame and wonder" (p. 124), a monument to the greed and entitlement of another age—though an age perhaps no worse than ours.

Susan's first impulse is to chuck the stuffed animals out. She learns that her great-uncle was a member of a Rooseveltian hunting club, a group of wealthy men who competed for annual prizes for the most and best animals killed. Yet, curiously, as she roams through the rooms trying to understand the old man, the ghost of the mansion, she finds that her desire to dispose of the trophies "was fading: the longer she lived with them the greater their hold" (p. 81). She begins to rearrange the specimens, and to have the taxidermy repaired. Thinking back to her own childhood love of museums, she feels that she now has "what she hadn't recognized back then: an air of permanence and contentment, the happy captivity of precious things" (p. 150). She now believes that "the dead were almost as beautiful as the living, sometimes more so. They had fewer needs" (p. 182). She has become, in fact, the sole curator of the museum—if not its prisoner.

But the haunted house has more secrets. She learns from an ancient survivor of the Hunt Club—a diplomat who had known Teddy Roosevelt—that her great uncle prided himself most on his "legacy," a project that does not seem synonymous with the galleries she has seen. But the Gothic inversion of "legacy" is "curse."

Susan has discovered plans for the house that show an extensive basement beneath it. There is no door to the basement in the house. But there is a steel manhole cover over a concrete plug in the garden, far from the house. Heavy equipment is required to uncover a shaft down to a tunnel. Going down this rabbit hole in her garden, Susan enters the basement wonderland and, like Alice, confronts a dodo. The galleries under the house are exhibits of animals that have become extinct. The boundary between the upper and lower galleries is the frontier earlier encountered by T: the diminishing natural world of the present and the world that was but is lost.

Yet there is more. Susan makes another descent into the rabbit hole, this time at night and drunk, while her concerned new boyfriend Jim calls after her from the shaft's mouth. She opens the door to a gallery yet unvisited and finds cabinets full of bones and artifacts, relics of indigenous peoples, mostly in Latin America, who are now extinct. We recall the Mayan group that was cluster-bombed in *Ghost Lights*.

What is Susan's response? As the novel ends, she is talking to Jim in her mind: "I'll walk through the rooms and you can come with me. Here's our ticket: now let's go in. Let's walk along the velvet rope and never touch the specimens. Stay with me, Jim. There's still some time. We'll keep each other company. Stay in these rooms for years and years, live on forever in a glorious museum" (p. 255). There are echoes here of Stephen King's *The Shining* (1977, film by Stanley Kubrick, 1980), and of Shirley Jackson's great novel, *The Haunting of Hill House* (1959). Susan has become not just the curator of the museum but also its final exhibit. And this is appropriate, since the most numerous species that will be lost in the Sixth Extinction will be ourselves.

As a California frontier Gothic saga, Millet's trilogy is indeed about encounters in the wilderness that are "intrinsically metaphysical and charged with paradox and emotional ambivalence." But we now understand that the greatest horror is not what the wilderness will do to us, but what we have done to it.

Endnotes

1   For surveys of Ecogothic, see Andrew Smith and William Hughes (eds.), *Ecogothic*, and Justin D. Edwards et al., eds., *Dark Scenes from a Damaged Earth*.
2   See, for example, Chandler's *The High Window*. David Ebershoff's *Pasadena: A Novel* is an adaptation of *Wuthering Heights* set in early twentieth-century Pasadena.

WORKS CITED

Akins, Damon B., and William J. Bauer, Jr. *We Are the Land: A History of Native California*. U of California P, 2021.

Anderson, Ross. "America's Atlantis." *The Atlantic Monthly*, October 2021, pp. 72–81.

Anger, Kenneth. *Hollywood Babylon*. Dell, 1981.

Austin, Mary. "A Poet in Outland," *The Overland Monthly and Out West Magazine*, Nov. 1927, p. 331+.

Austin, Mary. *A Woman of Genius*. Boston, 1917.

Bakker, Elna. *An Island Called California: An Ecological Introduction to Its Natural Communities*. 1971. U of California P, 1984.

Baym, Nina. *Women Writers of the West: 1833–1927*. U of Illinois P, 2011.

Bergland, Renée. *The National Uncanny: Indian Ghosts and American Subjects*. University P of New England, 2000.

Bierce, Ambrose. "The Death of Halpin Frayser." *The Complete Short Stories of Ambrose Bierce*. Ed. Ernest J. Hopkins. U of Nebraska P, 1984, pp. 58–72.

Bierce, Ambrose. "The Haunted Valley." *Complete Short Stories*, pp. 115–26.

Bierce, Ambrose. "An Inhabitant of Carcosa." *Complete Short Stories*, pp. 51–54.

Blunt, Katherine. *California Burning: The Fall of Pacific Gas and Electric and What It Means for America's Power Grid*. Penguin Random House, 2022.

Bradford, William. *Of Plymouth Plantation*. Ed. Harold Paget. E. P. Dutton, 1920.

Brophy, Robert J. *Robinson Jeffers*. Western Writers Series. Boise State U P, 1975.

Butler, Octavia E. *Parable of the Sower*. Four Walls Eight Windows, 1993.

Cartwright, Frederick F., and Michael Biddiss. *Disease in History: From Ancient Times to Covid 19*. 4th ed. Lume Books, 2020.

Chandler, Raymond. *The Big Sleep*. 1939. *The Raymond Chandler Omnibus*. Modern Library, 1975, pp. 1–139.

Chandler, Raymond. *The Lady in the Lake*. 1943. *Omnibus*, pp. 471–625.

Crow, Charles L., ed. *A Companion to American Gothic*. Chichester: Wiley Blackwell, 2014.

Crow, Charles L. *A Companion to the Regional Literatures of America*. Blackwell, 2003.

Crow, Charles L. "Homecoming in the California Visionary Romance." *Western American Literature* 24, Spring 1989, pp. 3–19.

Davidson, Cathy N., ed. *Critical Essays on Ambrose Bierce*. G. K. Hall, 1982.

Davidson, Cathy N. *The Experimental Fiction of Ambrose Bierce*. U of Nebraska P, 1984.

Davis, Mike. *Ecology of Fear: Los Angeles and the Imagination of Disaster*. Henry Holt, 1998.

Dawson, Emma Frances. *An Itinerant House and Other Stories*. San Francisco, 1897.

Didion, Joan. *Slouching Towards Bethlehem*. Dell, 1968.

Downey, Dara. *American Women's Ghost Stories in the Gilded Age*. Palgrave Macmillan, 2014.

Ebershoff, David. *Pasadena: A Novel*. Random House, 2002.

Edwards, Justin D., Rune Graulund, and Johan Hoglund, ed. *Dark Scenes from Damaged Earth: The Gothic Anthropocene.* U of Minnesota P, 2022.

Elroy, James. *My Dark Places.* Knopf, 1996.

Faflak, Joel, and Jason Haslam, ed. *American Gothic Culture.* Edinburgh UP, 2016.

Fine, David. "Film Noir and the Gothic." Crow, *Companion to American Gothic*, 2014. pp. 475–87.

Fitzgerald, F. Scott. "My Generation." *F. Scott Fitzgerald: A Short Autobiography.* Ed. James L. W. West III. Scribner, 2011, pp. 154–62.

Forbes, Jack B. *Columbus and Other Cannibals: The Wétiko Disease of Exploitation, Imperialism and Terrorism.* Seven Stories Press, 2008.

French, Nora May. *The Outer Gate: The Collected Poems of Nora May French.* Ed. Donald Sidney-Fryer and Alan Gullette. Hippocampus Press, 2009.

Freudenheim, Leslie Mendelson, and Elisabeth Sacks Sussman. *Building with Nature: Roots of the San Francisco Bay Region Tradition.* Peregrine Smith, 1974.

Gee, Alastair, and Dani Anguiano. *Fire in Paradise: An American Tragedy.* Norton, 2020.

Haslam, Jason. "Slavery and the American Gothic: The Ghost of the Future." Faflak and Haslam, 2016. pp. 44–59.

Hancocks, David. *A Different Nature: The Paradoxical World of Zoos and Their Uncertain Future.* U of California P, 2001.

Haraway, Donna. *Primate Visions: Gender, Race, and Nature in the World of Modern Science.* Routledge, 1989.

Hogle, Jerrold E., ed. *The Cambridge Companion to Modern Gothic.* Cambridge UP, 2014.

Holliday, J. S. The World Rushed In: The California Gold Rush Experience. Simon & Schuster, 1981.

Jeffers, Robinson. *Selected Poems.* Vintage, 1963.

Johnson, Denis. *Already Dead: A California Gothic.* Harper, 1997.

Johnson, Lizzie. *Paradise: One Town's Struggle to Survive an American Wildfire.* Random House, 2021.

Joshi, S. T., *The Weird Tale: Arthur Machen, Lord Dunsany, Algernon Blackwood, M. R. James, Ambrose Bierce, H. P. Lovecraft.* U of Texas P, 1990.

Kilston, Lyra. *Sun Seekers: The Cure of California.* Atelier, 2019.

Kingston, Maxine Hong. *Tripmaster Monkey: His Fake Book.* Knopf, 1989.

Kolbert, Elizabeth. *The Sixth Extinction: An Unnatural History.* Henry Holt, 2014.

Kolodny, Annette. "Letting Go Our Grand Obsessions: Notes toward a New Literary History of the American Frontiers." *American Literature* 64, March 1992, pp. 1–18. Reprinted in Crow, *Regional Literatures*, Blackwell, 2003, pp. 42–56.

Lim, Dennis. *David Lynch: The Man from Another Place.* Houghton Mifflin Harcourt, 2015.

London, Jack. *The Scarlet Plague.* Macmillan, 1912.

London, Jack, *The Valley of the Moon.* Peregrine Smith, 1975. 2 vols.

Macdonald, Ross. *The Underground Man. Ross Macdonald: Four Later Novels.* Ed. Tom Nolan. Library of America, 2017, pp. 653–881.

Melville, Herman. *Moby-Dick. Redburn, White-Jacket, Moby-Dick.* Ed. Thomas Tanselle. Library of America, 1983, pp. 771–1408.

Millet, Lydia. *Ghost Lights.* Norton, 2011.

Millet, Lydia. *How the Dead Dream.* Houghton Mifflin Harcourt, 2009.

Millet, Lydia. *Magnificence.* Norton, 2013.

Mogen, David, Scott P. Sanders, and Joanne B. Karpinski, ed. *Frontier Gothic: Terror and Wonder at the Frontier in American Literature.* Associated U Presses, 1993.

Murphy, Bernice M. *The California Gothic in Fiction and Film*. Edinburgh UP. 2022.

Murphy, Bernice M. *The Rural Gothic in American Popular Culture: Backwoods Horror and Terror in the Wilderness*. Palgrave Macmillan, 2013.

Norris, Frank. *Vandover and the Brute*. 1914. U of Nebraska P, 1978.

Nowak-McNeice, Katarzyna, and Agata Zarzycka, ed. *A Dark California: Essays on Dystopian Depictions in Popular Culture*. McFarland, 2017.

Nunn, Kem. *The Dogs of Winter*. Scribner, 1997.

Poe, Edgar Allan. "The Imp of the Perverse." *Edgar Allan Poe: Poetry and Tales*. Ed. Patrick F. Quinn. Library of America, 1984, pp. 826–32.

Polk, Dora Beale. *The Island of California: A History of the Myth*. U of Nebraska. P., 1991.

Prendergast, Catherine. *The Gilded Edge*. Dutton, 2021.

Procházka, Martin. *Ruins in the New World*. Litteraria Pragensia Books, 2012.

Purdy, Helen Throop. "Emma Frances Dawson." *California Historical Society Quarterly* 5, March 1926, p. 87.

Reisner, Mark. *A Dangerous Place: California's Unsettling Fate*. Pantheon, 2003.

Ringel, Faye *New England's Gothic Literature*. Edwin Mellen, 1995.

Scruggs, Charles. "American Film Noir." Hogle, 2014. pp. 123–37.

Showalter, Elaine. "Syphilis, Sexuality, and the Fiction of the Fin de Siècle." *Sex, Politics and Science in the Nineteenth-Century Novel*. Ed. Ruth Bernard Yeazell. Johns Hopkins UP, 1986, pp. 88–115.

Smith, Andrew, and William Hughes, editors. *Ecogothic*. Manchester UP, 2013.

Solnit, Rebecca. *Savage. Dreams: A Journey into the Hidden Wars of the American West*. U of California P, 1994.

Soltysik Monnet, Agnieszka. "They Are Legend." Crow, *Companion to American Gothic*. 2014. 212–22.

Sontag, Susan. *Illness as Metaphor and AIDS and Its Metaphors*. Picador, 1989.

Starr, Kevin *California: A History*. Modern Library, 2005.

Starr, Kevin. *Embattled Dreams: California in War and Peace 1940–1950*. Oxford UP, 2002.

Starr, Kevin. *Endangered Dreams: The Great Depression in California*. Oxford UP, 1996.

Stegner, Wallace. "California: The Experimental Society." *Saturday Review*, 23 Sept. 1967. p. 28.

Stein, William Bysshe. "'The Death of Halpin Frayser': The Poetics of Gothic Consciousness." *Critical Essays on Ambrose Bierce*. Ed. Cathy N. Davidson. G. K. Hall, 1982, pp. 217–27.

Steinbeck, John. *To a God Unknown*. Penguin, 1975.

Sterling, George. *The Thirst of Satan: Poems of Fantasy and Terror by George Sterling*. Edited by S. T. Joshi, Hippocampus Press, 2003.

Stewart, George R. *Earth Abides*. 1949. Del Rey, 1976.

Stewart, George R. *Ordeal by Hunger: The Story of the Donner Party*. Houghton Mifflin, 1936.

Talley, Sharon. "Anxious Representations of Uncertain Masculinity: The Failed Journey to Self-Understanding in Ambrose Bierce's 'The Death of Halpin Frayser.'" *The Journal of Men's Studies* 14, Spring 2006, pp. 161–72.

Tarnoff, Ben. *The Bohemians: Mark Twain and the San Francisco Writers Who Invented American Literature*. Penguin, 2014.

Tennyson, Alfred Lord. *Tennyson's Poetical Works*. Houghton Mifflin, 1898.

Walker, Franklin. *San Francisco's Literary Frontier*. U of Washington P., 1939.

Walker, Franklin. *The Seacoast of Bohemia*. Peregrine Smith, 1973.

Watkins, Claire Vaye. *Gold Fame Citrus*. Riverhead Books, 2015.

Weinstock, Jeffrey Andrew. "American Vampires." *American Gothic Culture*. Faflak and Haslam, 2016. pp. 213–14.

Whitman, Walt. *Whitman: Complete Poetry and Selected Prose*. Ed. Justin Kaplan. Library of America, 1982.

Willis, Connie. Introduction. *Earth Abides*. Ed. George R. Stewart. Ballantine, 2006, pp. xiii–xiv.

Wood, Robin. *Hitchcock's Films Revisited: Revised Edition*. Columbia UP, 2002.

Zola, Emile. *Nana*. Translated by George Holden. Penguin, 1972.

AFTERWORD

Facing west from California's shores, Walt Whitman asked, "But where is what I started for so long ago, and why is it yet unfound? (p. 267). Unable to answer these questions, Californians have remade their state again and again. At times it has seemed complete, as, for example, in 1940, when according to Kevin Starr (1940–2017), its network of new roads and bridges and a water supply adequate for a maturing California made it "a unity achieved by public works." (*Endangered*, p. 339).

Then again, the world rushed in during WWII, unmaking and remaking everything. More recently, the tech industry of Silicon Valley created tens of thousands of new jobs, changing not only the state's but the nation's economy, as completely as did the California gold rush.

And still, as scholars Katarzyna Nowak-McNeice and Agata Zarzyka recently observed, "California does not make sense" (p. 3). A flippant response would be that it must make pretty good sense for the forty million citizens who have chosen to live here and who have built an economy that is the fourth or fifth largest in the world.

Nowak-McNeice and Zarzycka have a point, however. The narrative that we Californians tell ourselves, as the above chapters have tried to show, has been constructed by suppressing much of the story. The California dream, in its various evolutions, is maintained by omission and forgetting. What is repressed or ignored returns in the California Gothic. Yet it would be a mistake to make California a scapegoat for all that is wrong in the United States or the world. Jeremiads about the failure of California, often with pictures of the homeless in San Francisco, Oakland, and Los Angeles, can be read in the media every day and are themselves willful suppressions of shared national shortcomings. Some sixty years ago, Wallace Stegner summed up the dynamic between California and the rest of the nation thus: "Like the rest of America, California is unformed, innovative, ahistorical, hedonistic, acquisitive, and energetic, only more so." (p. 28). The quotation is often given in an abbreviated form, in a way that stresses the difference between California and the rest of the country: California exaggerates, is extreme.

The full passage, with its catalog of shared qualities, indicates the common ground: not different, only intensified.

Which is to say that the California Dream is only a version of the American Dream, and California shares its Gothic nightmares with the rest of the country. And perhaps, as we look west from California's shores toward Asia, we should recognize that we share dreams and nightmares with the world. The great challenges of disease, climate change, and societal collapse are shared with everyone, and the same dystopian nightmares await all continents. California Gothic sounds a warning for the world.

INDEX

Milton Keynes UK
Ingram Content Group UK Ltd.
UKHW011818221223
434865UK00001B/21